DREAM Up NOW

THE Teen Journal FOR CREATIVE Self-Discovery

Rayne Lacko

with community outreach advisor Lesley Holmes

free spirit
PUBLISHING®

Text copyright © 2020 by Rayne Lacko

All rights reserved under International and Pan-American Copyright Conventions. Unless otherwise noted, no part of this book may be reproduced, stored in a retrieval system, or transmitted in any form or by any means, electronic, mechanical, photocopying, recording, or otherwise, without express written permission of the publisher, except for brief quotations or critical reviews. For more information, go to freespirit.com/permissions.

Free Spirit, Free Spirit Publishing, and associated logos are trademarks and/or registered trademarks of Free Spirit Publishing Inc. A complete listing of our logos and trademarks is available at freespirit.com.

Library of Congress Cataloging-in-Publication Data
Names: Lacko, Rayne, author.
Title: Dream up now : the teen journal for creative self-discovery / Rayne Lacko, with community
    outreach advisor Lesley Holmes.
Description: Minneapolis, MN : Free Spirit Publishing, Inc., [2020]
Identifiers: LCCN 2020013096 | ISBN 9781631985492 (paperback)
Subjects: LCSH: Emotions in adolescence—Juvenile literature. | Self-realization—Juvenile literature. |
    Diaries—Authorship—Juvenile literature.
Classification: LCC BF724.3.E5 .L33 2020 | DDC 155.5/124—dc23
LC record available at https://lccn.loc.gov/2020013096

Free Spirit Publishing does not have control over or assume responsibility for author or third-party websites and their content. At the time of this book's publication, all facts and figures cited within are the most current available. All telephone numbers, addresses, and website URLs are accurate and active; all publications, organizations, websites, and other resources exist as described in this book; and all have been verified as of February 2020. If you find an error or believe that a resource listed here is not as described, please contact Free Spirit Publishing. Parents, teachers, and other adults: We strongly urge you to monitor children's use of the internet.

Reading Level HS-Adult; Interest Level Ages 13 & up;
Fountas & Pinnell Guided Reading Level Z+

Edited by Cassie Sitzman
Cover and interior design by Shannon Pourciau

10 9 8 7 6 5 4 3 2 1
Printed in the United States of America
V20300820

Free Spirit Publishing Inc.
6325 Sandburg Road, Suite 100
Minneapolis, MN 55427-3674
(612) 338-2068
help4kids@freespirit.com
freespirit.com

FSC
www.fsc.org
MIX
Paper from
responsible sources
FSC® C005010

Free Spirit offers competitive pricing.
Contact edsales@freespirit.com for pricing information on multiple quantity purchases.

DEDICATION

My gratitude to all the young people who've trusted me with their words and art, especially my own children. For all those who dare to create, may you find much more than you thought possible within you.

—R. L.

For Sienna and Nya, may your creativity continue to make you soar!

—L. H.

Gratitude to the Experts

Just as every young person has his/her/their own path to self-expression, the many successful and creative adults who contributed to this guided journal have each found a way to employ creativity to resolve difficult emotions and harness the power of positive emotions to build a beautiful life. We are indebted to these kind-hearted people: Korum Bischoff, Sara Bourland, Melissa Dinwiddie, Tanesha "Ksyn" Cason, Antonio Manuel Chavira, Angie Godfrey, André Hardy, Lauryn J. Hunter, Shelley Klammer, Lisa Manterfield, Ryan "Bodhi" Marcus, MaLee Muse, Courtney Oliver, Rich Redmond, Gem Seddon, Stacie Shewmake, Kristin Tollefson, Sann Wilder, and VH1 Save the Music Foundation.

Contents

BONUS PAGES

To download additional bonus pages and a leadership guide, visit freespirit.com/dream.

Foreword
by Sann Wilder

I am no stranger to loss. For years, that numb hollowness was a closer companion to me than my own family. However, I am fortunate enough to be able to use the past tense when talking about those times.

When I was 10 years old, my family suffered a house fire. We lost nearly everything we owned, and our two cats and dogs were killed in the inferno. Two weeks later, we moved halfway across the country, and I lost any support I might have had. I could have turned to my parents, of course, but they were suffering just as much as I was. So I turned to the arts.

The ability to use art to give shape to your emotions, to describe them, to place them somewhere outside so they are not contained in the mind—that might be the greatest power a person can have. If I could look at my writing and my art, at my thoughts given form, then I knew my grief was real and I could begin to heal. I wrote down things I hadn't even realized I was feeling. By transcribing my loss, I was able to move past it. And I discovered something I'd never truly known: peace.

The world is so beautiful. We have towering forests and delicate, lace-like flowers and freshly painted skies. We have kind people with bright eyes and dazzling smiles that sparkle like stars. The arts help me remember that no emotion is permanent, and knowing that grief is not permanent helps me get through it. The journal in your hands is filled with creative activities that can help you understand and deal with whatever you're feeling. It helped me, and I hope it will help you too.

—Sann Wilder, 16

Introduction
by Lauryn J. Hunter

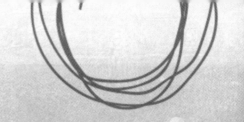

As an art therapist working with teens, I integrate art, music, and dance to help release tension or stress in the body. A creative outlet can be a safe and easy way to open a conversation and learn more about a person's physical, mental, and emotional well-being. As a specialist in human development, I focus on repairing broken attachments in relationships, such as grief, adoption, addiction, trauma, and divorce of parents. In my 15 years' experience working in community mental health and facilitating art therapy groups, the one thing I have noticed most is the resiliency of young people, especially when you're enjoying feelings of safety, trust, love, support, and acceptance.

Feelings related to fear and stress may cause a person to feel physically sick, depressed, or anxious. Social media and cyberbullying can cause many teens to feel pressure to be or act a certain way. Subliminal messages about identity, body image, and self-expression sometimes leave out celebrating what makes people unique and special. It is natural to struggle with the concept of *Who am I in this big world?* What you see and experience at home, at school, and in your community impacts your personal identity, self-esteem, and social skills.

Managing and sorting through the many feelings you have throughout the day can sometimes feel very uncomfortable in the body. Some teens try to regulate these feelings with impulsive behavior, self-harm, or substance abuse. *Dream Up Now* can provide huge relief for anyone struggling with their feelings and thoughts. This journal is full of safe activities you can do on your own, wherever you feel safe to open up and explore your feelings in privacy. Through the guided activities, you will learn the importance of asking for help and that it's perfectly normal to have more than one feeling at a time. These activities can even help you find ways to improve your grades, friendships, and self-image.

This journal is a great way to build your self-awareness by keeping track of your feelings and how negative or positive feelings impact your behavior. What makes *Dream Up Now* unique is its collaborative approach. Trustworthy, caring adults who have found success through their own creativity provide you with tools and activities to help you figure out what's going on right now and use your natural, inborn talents to express yourself. By exploring your feelings in your *Dream Up Now* creative journal, you'll begin your journey of self-discovery. The most valuable part of this journal, and the part that creates healing, comes from you being honest with yourself. No one has to see what you've created—unless you choose to share it. Each activity focuses on a different identified feeling. By journaling, drawing, listening to music, and creating, you'll learn how to take time for yourself, practice self-care, and self-regulate in the moment to feel more comfortable in your body. The activities ignite self-awareness, helping you realize that you are part of a greater community, you are not alone, and you can make a difference when you find ways to collaborate with others and become a community leader.

My favorite message throughout *Dream Up Now* is this: there is no "wrong" way to be creative. As long as you allow yourself to *try*, to experience the process, and to move through challenging feelings, you will feel better.

—*Lauryn J. Hunter, L.M.F.T., A.T.R.,* is an award-winning art therapist offering powerful ways to improve one's physical, mental, and emotional well-being.

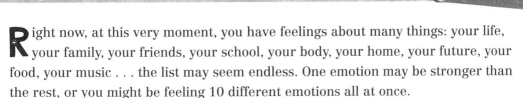

A Note to you
from the Author

Right now, at this very moment, you have feelings about many things: your life, your family, your friends, your school, your body, your home, your future, your food, your music . . . the list may seem endless. One emotion may be stronger than the rest, or you might be feeling 10 different emotions all at once.

Or maybe you were feeling super chill and zen, and then a crappy memory popped into your thoughts and now you find yourself replaying that scene over and over in your head. I understand that you have feelings about that scene. But what do you *do* with them?

Dream Up Now has creative solutions to help you deal with the darkest lows. Even better, it shows you how to use the power of a good day to make your life go the way you want. I believe that if you're experiencing feelings of happiness, of confidence, and of power, then you're in the perfect state of mind to begin building the life you want to live.

You might be wondering: *Isn't feeling happy good enough?* That's a fair question. Feeling happy *is* good. But happiness isn't the be-all, end-all destination. It's what you *do* with these positive feelings that brings real change.

Lucky for you, you've found *Dream Up Now.* This guided journal offers plenty of ideas for getting the things you want in life.

My friend Lesley Holmes and I work with many teens, and what we've noticed is that making art alleviates pain, whether you see yourself as an artist or not. It also can bond you with others, because if you dare to share your art, you give people an opportunity to care about you. Writing, drawing, and listening to music help you realize what is going on inside, *really* going on—the truth. Lesley and I wanted to give teens more opportunities to explore their inner worlds, and that's how this guided journal came to be.

When Lesley and I first met in 2015, music united us. (If you've ever bonded with someone over your favorite songs, you know what I'm talking about.) Lesley represented a music therapy nonprofit, and I was writing books and magazine articles about how music, especially when shared among friends, can truly heal. The first inklings of *Dream Up Now* were centered in resolving emotional struggles using music therapy methods. But we recognized that each person has an individual approach to self-expression. Music is universal, the cornerstone of every culture and age—but so are creative writing, drawing, and movement. As a teen, you have so much to say, and you have the power to express yourself. We believe you have the right and privilege to dream up your own art—now.

Dream Up Now was created because your feelings are valuable. All your feelings—the light ones, the dark ones, the weird ones, the dangerous ones, the so-happy-you-might-explode ones, the please-put-me-out-of-my-misery ones—make up who you are.

Lesley and I have read the research about the power of art and alternative therapies, and we work directly with teens and with educators and therapists from a variety of fields. We know about all the benefits of leading a creative life.*

But beyond its benefits, I believe that art was born of the very human need to express who you are. Art gives you the words you may find impossible to say. It gives you a language all humans can understand. Art allows you to play, and play is how you first navigated the big, unknown world before you could put a name to your feelings, let alone explore them.

Art gives you an opportunity to take a painful memory and pluck it out of your head and stick it on the page (or in a song, or a drawing, or even blow it away with your breath). Once that scene is out, and all the emotions tied to it come out as well, it loses its power to hurt you.

Art gives you freedom to use your hands, and hands are always looking for something meaningful to do. Creating something that represents a portion of your inner world is probably the most rewarding thing you can do with them.

You are an artist. You are. Go ahead and put that on your college application, your résumé, or your social media profile, because it's true. You were born to *create*. Your daydreams, your deepest wishes, your choice of clothes to wear, and songs to listen to, and preferred routes to walk from one place to another—these are all tiny revelations of yourself as an artist.

If you've ever thought about how you wish your bedroom looked, or how you would design or choreograph a music video, or what song you wish you'd written or could perform, or if you have a favorite dance move, or a preference for wearing a certain color, or a character you like to doodle, know that those thoughts are evidence of your self-expression. You are yourself a unique creation. There is no one quite like you.

---

*In fact, according to a 2014 study from the President's Committee on the Arts and the Humanities, high school students involved in the arts are four times more likely to be recognized for academic achievement, yet many schools are cutting the arts. If you want to find out more about how you can start an arts club or music program at your school, see the online leadership guide. Visit freespirit.com/dream to download.

The creative activities you'll find in this journal were designed by successful adults who have dealt with the same emotions you're experiencing now and who used various artistic means to deal with the struggles common to teen life.

You will find that these writers care about you and your well-being. And no, they don't know you. Neither do I. But we are sharing the workings of our hearts, the secret hurts of our pasts, and the advice we wish someone had given us, because we want to help you create the life you want to live. You are not alone.

Your creativity is your ticket to making your life go the way you want. And there's a good chance you'll enjoy the process along the way.

—*Rayne Lacko*

How to Use This Creative Journal

The journal in your hands is easy to explain, and even easier to use. How do you feel right now? Flip through the book and find the emotion that best fits your current feeling. Or browse the emotions listed in the contents if you need some help choosing where to begin. If you're feeling something people might describe as "dark" or "bad" or "negative," please know that your feelings are safe here. Or maybe you've had "bad" feelings in the past and are ready to sort them out today.

Relief comes with the realization that every dark emotion has a companion, a "light" emotion. Both are normal and can happen any time to anyone. Once you've faced your darkness, you can drag it out into the light and use art to change it in whatever way best serves you. This guided journal is your creative tool to turn your darkness(es) into light.

Use your *Dream Up Now* journal whenever you want—or need—to sort out what's going on in your world. It's here for you on your best days. And it's here for you in your most difficult times. *Dream Up Now* can help you create the life you want to live.

Explore the sets of light and dark emotions as needed—or make a plan to focus on specific pairs of feelings if you feel ready to take control.

In each emotion section, you'll find a short introduction about the contributing writer. Then, you'll hear from the writer themselves. They might share about an experience with the emotion or tell you about the role creativity plays in their life. Finally, they share an activity where you'll use your own creativity to work through the emotion and learn more about yourself.

Write or doodle in the margins. Underline sentences you want to remember. This journal belongs to you, so make it your own.

Emotions change, sometimes unexpectedly. Once you complete a dark emotion activity, you are welcome to move right into the light emotion that is paired with it. Keep in mind that sometimes resolving one dark emotion uncovers another one. Move through your *Dream Up Now* guided journal by tuning into your feelings. Do the activities in whatever order feels right to you. The good news is that whatever difficulty you are going through, there is a corresponding light emotion available to you. Try to keep exploring the emotions until you can complete a light emotion activity. Always go from darkness into light.

Some of what you'll find in *Dream Up Now* is not, at first glance, an art project. You may find an activity about getting organized or about figuring out how to get a good night's sleep. You might wonder, *Is this art?* The answer is yes, it is. It's art because it requires your creativity. It's art because you are designing your life to go the way you want it to go. You are taking control of your emotions to make your life better, more playful, happier.

> *Dream Up Now* can even help you find friends. Making art and mindfully creating the kind of life you want builds authenticity. When you're honest about who you are, you naturally attract your kind of people. Sharing your art helps you learn the lifelong skill of opening yourself to others and establishing trust—a solid start for any relationship. Art builds community. You can share your art @dreamupnowjournal #dreamupnow.

Here's a tip for working in *Dream Up Now*: watch for repeats. As you complete activities, what topics, people, or events do you keep mentioning? What words do you tend to use the most? Which emotions trigger the most discomfort, and which are you working the hardest to feel more often?

Emotion sets can be read and completed one time—or 100 times. As your circumstances change, your feelings change. If you land on a page that you've already completed, take a moment to review it. Is it still true?

Reflect on the answers you gave and make changes as needed. When you redo an activity, you may get a completely different outcome. As you begin using art to manage your emotions, you'll gain wisdom. Need more space to create? Take your creativity outside this journal and into a notebook or sketchbook. Expand on or repeat an activity, elaborate on a writing prompt, make plans for the future, doodle, or create more pieces of art.

Every day, you're growing, learning, and changing. This means that however you feel, right this instant, is impermanent. It's absolutely going to change, and changing emotions are okay because every emotion is valuable.

You are invited to create, to transform your darkest hours into the life you want to live. Begin now. How do you feel?

I FEEL . . . TIRED

mental numbness / wishing for comfort / inability to focus / loss of motivation

Meet Courtney Oliver

Trying to balance being who you want to be and fitting in is tough. "It is important to give yourself time to figure out who you are," Courtney says. "There can be a lot of trial and error." It is also difficult when parents, family members, and friends want you to be a certain way even though sometimes you want to be different. Feeling tired, she says, affects our decision-making and mood. She finds it helpful to use the acronym HALT before making a decision—checking in with herself to see if she is hungry, angry, lonely, or tired. If she can say yes to any of these, Courtney knows it is probably not the best time to make a decision and will try to resolve her feelings first.

Courtney has worked with teens as a counselor for over 12 years. She currently works directly with teens at Bainbridge Youth Services (BYS) as a licensed mental health counselor and chemical dependency professional. Through her work, Courtney helps teens struggling with depression, anxiety, and relationship issues develop a positive self-image and create a life they love and deserve. Learn more about Courtney at askbys.org.

Courtney Shares

Lack of sleep affects everyone. It can change our mood and our focus and can create mental numbness and loss of interest in life. Lack of sleep also plays with our brain. Thinking things are worse than they are, we can become overwhelmed by the small things. As life happens, it is easy to get distracted by deadlines, stress, and/or excitement, which can cause us not to get to bed on time or to create unhealthy bedtime routines.

DREAM UP NOW

This activity helps you create a nighttime routine and set yourself up for a good night's sleep. Having a bedtime routine and a restful environment is important because it tells your brain it is time to go to bed.

When creating a bedtime routine, remember this acronym: *Nighttime is the SLOWEST part of the day.*

S—Scribbling/journaling. Journaling or scribbling in a notebook can help your brain unwind and relax. Search for "night journaling prompts" online to find ideas. Examples of prompts include making a gratitude list or writing about what brought you joy for the day. Make sure you place items such as a notebook and pencils you like by your bed for easy access.

L—List (to-do list for the next day). It is hard to sleep if you are thinking about all the things you need to do tomorrow. Make a to-do list to get it off your mind. You can either write your list on paper or email it to yourself. Start making your list *at least one hour before bed* and make sure you give yourself at least five minutes of devoted time to write everything.

O—Off (screens off). Experts say it is beneficial to be off all screens for at least 30 minutes to one hour before bed, but the more time, the better.* Start by staying off screens for 30 minutes before going to sleep. If you are a person who enjoys bingeing on streaming TV or scrolling through the internet before bed, try listening to music or meditating instead. Or you can read a book or magazine (not school-related) that is not on an electronic device. Make sure the room is completely dark for the deepest sleep.

W—Wash/hygiene. If you don't already have a bathroom routine, get one! It helps tell your body it is time to go to sleep. Washing your face can represent washing off the day and can help transition your mind to thoughts of bed. Brushing your teeth can symbolize the end of eating for the day, which helps your body understand the day is done.

E—Extensions (Pilates and stretching). Taking time to stretch before bed reduces stress and helps improve sleep. Moving your body around can ease any aches or tightness that might have occurred during the day, so pain will not go to bed with you.

S—Silence/meditation. Spending some time being silent or meditating before bed can help you relax and feel connected to your body and can distract you from thoughts that disrupt sleep. A great breathing exercise to help with sleep and overall mental health is called 4-7-8 Breathing:

1. Exhale completely through your mouth while making a *whoosh* sound.
2. Close your mouth and inhale quietly through your nose to a mental count of four.

---

*According to the National Sleep Foundation. For more information about sleep, visit sleepfoundation.org.

3. Now hold your breath for a count of seven.

4. Exhale completely through your mouth, making another whoosh sound, for eight seconds.

5. Repeat the cycle three more times.

T—Temperature. Figure out what temperature feels comfortable for you. Create a log of days you sleep better and see if there are any patterns in temperature, what you were wearing, or how many blankets or covers you had.

Advice I Wish I'd Had
"You are the expert. You know yourself best."
—Courtney Oliver

I Feel . . . Tired

Personalize Courtney's *Nighttime is the SLOWEST part of the day* plan for your room, your rest, and your life. How can you make it your own?

S—Scribbling/journaling. Choose a few writing prompts to get started.

L—List (to-do list for the next day). What do you need to do tomorrow?

O—Off (screens off). Where will you put your devices so you won't be tempted? How long before bedtime will you try to stay off screens?

W—Wash/hygiene. What is your plan for a nighttime bathroom routine?

E—Extensions (Pilates and stretching). Write your favorite stretches.

S—Silence/meditation. Write down any intentions, questions, or concerns, just to get them out of your head.

T—Temperature. What's your preferred temperature for sleeping?

Share your art
@dreamupnowjournal
#dreamupnow.

I FEEL . . . FIRED UP

confidence / positive self-regard / gratitude /
fueling your positivity for down days

Meet Courtney Oliver

Courtney believes using creative expression can help improve your mood when you're feeling tired and motivate you when you're fired up. (For more about Courtney, see page 8.) She enjoys making art and listening to her favorite music. One of her favorite art forms is collage, the process of cutting out words and images that speak to you and arranging them on a page. Courtney shows you how to create a vision board, a collage of images and words that focus on (or help you visualize) how you want to feel and what you want to achieve. Visualization is a scientifically proven mind exercise Olympic athletes have used for decades to significantly improve or achieve new goals. On your vision board, you might place the word *love* over a picture of your pet or include an image of your dream job or a quote that inspires you. Layer your collage with your interests, goals, dreams, wants, and needs. When it is complete, look at it at least once a day as a gentle reminder to focus on the positive, and on what you want out of life or who you want to be. Creating a vision board is a fun process!

Courtney Shares

Feeling fired up is an opportunity to feel confident and motivate yourself in the right direction. It is important to utilize this emotion because when you're fired up, you probably feel like your best self and want to share it with the world. A vision board can help you start the dreaming process to create goals. When you feel fired up, a vision board helps you realign and focus on what you want. It can also remind you of what you're working toward when you are tired.

DREAM UP NOW

A vision board is made up of photos and words put together in a collage. People make vision boards for everything—from goals for who they want to become to what energy or things in life they want to attract.

Use the space on pages 14–15 to create a vision board. You'll need a glue stick, scissors, and photos and text. Your images can be cut from magazines or newspapers, found online, or photos you have taken yourself.

Here are some questions to ignite your imagination:

- What character traits would you like to be known for?
- What quotes inspire you?
- What do you want your life to look like?
- What places would you like to visit?
- How do you want to dress?
- What do you wish you had more time for in your life?
- What have you always wanted to do but have never had the courage to try?
- What matters most to you?
- What do you love?

Advice I Wish I'd Had
"Let your vision board be driven by your heart. Dream big to create your goals!"

—Courtney Oliver

I Feel . . . Fired Up

Share your art
@dreamupnowjournal
#dreamupnow.

I FEEL . . . PRESSURED

reacting to expectations / fear of failing / worry for the future

Meet Antonio Manuel Chavira

When Antonio was a teen, he felt overburdened at every turn. Growing up in a community- and church-oriented family in East LA, he had to take care of his brothers and his household and work two jobs. Often, he had to take care of his parents too. Finding time to himself, just to feel free and unconfined, was tough. He squeezed extra hours out of the middle of the night and stole away moments between classes or before returning home, trying to find breathing room anywhere he could. But the pressure to perform was always there, surrounding him at all times. "It felt like I was expected to do everything perfectly," he says. Being a teen involves pressure on all sides—you have to deal with social, personal, and educational expectations from a huge variety of people. "Personally, I could've done with a lot less of it."

Antonio's creativity influences several industries. In addition to being an author and a professor, he is the director of story and development at Massive Chaos—Design and Animation, and the VP of operations and marketing at RACAIA Architecture and Interior Design. Antonio has earned multiple screenplay awards at various film festivals, including Fantastic Planet Film Festival, NYC Independent Film Festival, and the World Series of Screenwriting. Learn more about Antonio at massivechaos.com.

Antonio Shares

Being a teen, for me, meant linking my actions and behavior to expected outcomes. Sometimes, the outcomes were as childish and unlikely to happen as that old rhyme, "Step on a crack and you'll break your mother's back." I'd think, "If I have money, I'll be okay." All I ended up doing was working harder and exhausting myself. "A degree will prove that I'm smart." Did it? I now have two bachelor's and two master's degrees, only to discover that all along I simply did not feel like a smart person.

Many believe, "I can make my partner or significant other happy by doing everything they say," when, in truth, we are all responsible for finding our own happiness. Through writing, I came to discover that many of my beliefs were only fables—things I thought were sure to happen but didn't quite turn out the way I expected, and instead helped me learn something new about myself and create my own path to happiness. Did tripping and falling on my face in public once suddenly make me an idiot? Did choking on a test, performance, or game mean that I would always let people down? Did breaking up with my girlfriend mean that my life was over and that I wasn't worthy of love? Of course not. We're only human, and we deserve the freedom to make mistakes. Lots of mistakes. Unlimited mistakes. More than that, we deserve endless benefit of the doubt for the future. Making a mistake (or many) never means we will always and only make mistakes in life. We deserve this generosity of understanding—the permission to fail sometimes so we can learn from our mistakes—especially from ourselves.

DREAM UP NOW

I'd like you to write your life story to this point as a fable. Whether your fable features an animal, a magical creature, or a human, the main character has the same background as you, thinks the same thoughts as you, and is dealing with the same pressures as you. But unlike the childhood stories you are familiar with, your fable will not hold back in describing the main character's challenges. Painful deaths, difficult relationships, abuse, exhaustion, frustration, loneliness—this main character understands intimately any experiences you have gone through. And on the other end, they will discover an essential, powerful lesson about life.

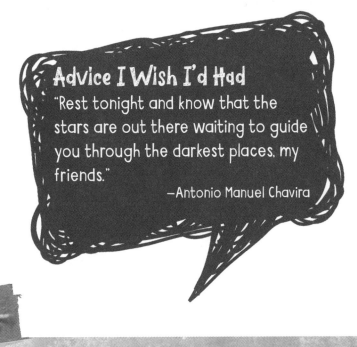

Advice I Wish I'd Had

"Rest tonight and know that the stars are out there waiting to guide you through the darkest places, my friends."

—Antonio Manuel Chavira

I Feel . . . Pressured

Tell your fable in four parts. Write as much as you can in each. This story is yours, so give yourself the space to write out every important detail.

1. **The Background.** This fable's main character has your background, which you know intimately. Write that out, being as epic in scale as you want—in fact, try to be even more epic.

2. **The Struggle.** In this part of your fable, your main character faces increasingly difficult life circumstances. What are they? How are they related to one another? What very terrible moments has the main character had to face? And what was the worst possible moment?

3. **The Return.** We now see everything that has led to the main character's present day. What must the main character learn in order to discover something true about themselves, overcome adversity, and complete their mythological journey?

4. **The Lesson.** Pretend you are a reader observing your character's experiences. Because this is a fable, what truth or life lesson can readers discover? How can they use this fable to overcome their own life obstacles? What wisdom can only you share through your story?

1. The Background

2. The Struggle

3. The Return

4. The Lesson

Share your art
@dreamupnowjournal
#dreamupnow.

I FEEL . . . HOPE

handling tough situations / making self-care a priority /
thinking before reacting

Meet Antonio Manuel Chavira

As a teen, Antonio sometimes felt totally overwhelmed. (For more about Antonio, see page 16.) Just about every night he had a hard time sleeping. So he'd stay up late, journaling and writing short (or very long) stories. This was the only way he felt that he could work through whatever he was dealing with that day and find hope—whether he was feeling angry at his parents, dealing with girlfriend issues, or just needing space to let his mind wander. At the time, he just wanted to write until he was tired enough to sleep. But in truth, what he needed most was the space to validate what he was going through.

Antonio Shares

When I was in high school, before I'd begin to write, I'd usually feel so overwhelmed that I didn't know what was going on inside me. Just writing things out for a few minutes was often enough to help me identify what was going on and feel more hopeful. If I felt in the flow when writing a story that was deeply tragic, I was probably dealing with something sad or tragic. If I was caught up in writing something furious, I was likely in an angry place. Most of the time, just getting it out and onto paper helped me sleep more soundly.

I wanted to express my feelings as large as they felt inside. A lot of my writing was tragic: lovers fighting against impossible odds and ultimately dying, a relationship between two people destroyed by family hierarchy, mental illness, or crushing social expectations. In short, I often opted for sadness, since I had a lot of sadness to work through.

Writing dramatic stories helped me work through the painful pressures coming from all sides. Putting my characters through impossible situations helped me come to terms with some of the very crushing expectations that were placed on me without blowing up at everyone in my life. Even better, I enjoyed writing. Even if it was midnight or two in the morning, writing was always there for me and gave me hope.

DREAM UP NOW

Let's dig into the dark fable you wrote in I Feel . . . Pressured to find out some secrets and truths about you. I've prepared a special quiz to reveal what is going on in your life and help you find solutions that work for you, and only you. Are you ready to reflect on your fable?

I Feel . . . Hope

Go back and reread your fable from I Feel . . . Pressured, knowing that your story was about you. The main character is you and everything they've gone through was real and true. Answer these questions with responses as short or as lengthy as you want.

> **TIP**: It can be helpful to mark up your fable on pages 18–19 as you think about these questions.

Does this story do justice to your own experience? Where does it fall short? Where is it especially on point?

Which events in the main character's background cause them to make decisions later in the story? How did these decisions work out for the character?

What's the most honorable part about this main character's journey?

What's the most painful part about the main character's journey?

What must the main character understand to grow? Why is it so hard for them to understand this lesson?

Were there any other things impacting the main character's difficulties, aside from the ones you wrote in the story?

How do you think this main character grew as a person after these painful experiences?

How did their struggles make the main character wiser and more understanding of others?

How do you imagine the main character will apply this life lesson to how they act from now on?

Is there anything you'd like to add to the story now?

If you were to write a brief follow-up to the main character's journey, what happens next? What insights help them grow even more?

Feel free to change your fable or add on to it. Does the lesson still apply? Or has it grown or changed?

Share your art
@dreamupnowjournal
#dreamupnow.

SECRET (AWESOME) FACTS ABOUT ME

Every time you open your *Dream Up Now* journal, write or sketch one thing that is cool or nice or interesting or unique about you.

TIP: It's okay to ask others for ideas.

Share your art @dreamupnowjournal #dreamupnow.

I FEEL . . . LOSS

death of a loved one, friend, or pet / divorce /
moving to a new home or school

Meet Lisa Manterfield

When Lisa was a teen, she struggled with figuring out where she fit in the world. She was lucky to find a great group of friends who were "nerdy like me," she says. "We didn't fit in and so we fit together." When her dad died unexpectedly, she was shocked and unprepared. She didn't know how to express her grief and didn't feel like talking to her family, worried that she might upset them more. Because she kept her feelings inside, it took a long time to come to terms with her dad's death. Her sadness kept coming back over and over again. She realized that loss could take many forms: "Sometimes you don't even realize it and you don't understand why you feel angry or sad or frustrated." To deal with these feelings, she got creative. "I loved anything related to storytelling. I was involved in theater, dance, and music, and of course, I wrote."

Lisa is an author of Young Adult novels, including *The Smallest Thing* and *A Strange Companion*. Her next book will be a YA thriller. Her teenaged main characters deal with many kinds of grief and loss. A writer for more than 20 years, Lisa is an Amazon best seller, a James Kirkwood Literary Prize nominee, a San Francisco Writing Contest finalist, and an SCBWI contest awardee. You can learn more about her at lisamanterfield.com.

Lisa Shares

When I was 15, my dad died suddenly. I thought I would feel sad, but instead I was angry and confused. I felt like I didn't belong in my own body anymore and that my friends no longer understood me. I wanted to climb out of my own skin and be someone else. As soon as I could, I moved to a new school. I ran away from my feelings.

What I learned is that all those feelings come from grief, and each of us feels grief in a unique way. Grief can make you want to scream or punch something or cry. It can also make you feel tired or sad or like you want to climb into bed and stay there forever.

I learned that losing a loved one isn't the only thing that can cause grief. If you've ever moved to a new neighborhood or changed schools, lost a friendship or seen your parents go through a divorce, or even had important plans for the future that didn't work out, those are all forms of loss too.

The hard part about some losses is that other people don't understand them. They might say things they think are helpful, but that only make you feel worse. They ask, "What's wrong?" and you can't tell them. You know how you feel, but you don't know why you feel that way. You might think, "Of course I'm sad my friend moved away, but why do I feel angry, scared, and lost?" Rather than talking about how you feel, you find yourself covering up your feelings and stuffing them away, so you don't have to try to explain them.

If you try to ignore your grief, as I did, sooner or later it will find you, and it won't want to leave. So let's create a way to get your feelings out and help you understand why you feel the way you do.

DREAM UP NOW

Writing a letter is a good way to process your grief about the person or thing you've lost. In a letter you can share dreams that weren't realized or things you wish you'd said or done. Getting these thoughts out of your head and onto the page can help you process them so you can move past them.

Advice I Wish I'd Had

"Be honest about how you feel."
—Lisa Manterfield

I Feel . . . Loss

Write a letter to the person or thing you've lost.

- Tell them how your life is different now.
- Tell them the things you'll no longer get to do.
- Tell them the plans for the future that will have to change.
- Tell them about how the loss has changed how you feel about yourself.

Write down everything you want to tell that person or thing. This letter is for your eyes only, unless you choose to share it, so be honest about your emotions, even if they seem silly or selfish, or are something others think you shouldn't feel. Your loss is your own, and it's okay to feel however you do. If you need more help or would like someone to talk to about your loss, reach out to a hotline or app listed in the resource section at the end of this journal.

Dear _____,

Share your art
@dreamupnowjournal
#dreamupnow.

I FEEL . . . PEACE

letting go / finding healing / taking steps into the unknown / reframing what happened

Meet Lisa Manterfield

When Lisa was dealing with her dad's death, she used to dance. When she felt angry or frustrated, or when she had some other emotion she couldn't express in words, she would put on music—something dramatic, like Queen's "Bohemian Rhapsody"—and dance out her feelings. "I'd do leaps and twists and run as fast as I could into a jump until I'd burned through all those feelings. I'd be breathless afterward, but that breathing also helped me feel calm again," she says. It's a lot easier to think through problems when you're not angry or frustrated. (For more about Lisa, see page 27.)

Lisa Shares

When you lose something valuable or someone you love, it can take a long time before you stop feeling sad. After my dad died it was several years before I could talk about him without feeling my chest tighten and my voice crack. But during that time, I had to keep moving forward with my life. I went to college, got my first real job, and even got married, but I wasn't ready to do all that right away. First, I had to feel ready to move on.

When someone dies, we have ways to say goodbye. We celebrate the person's life, hold a funeral and perhaps a vigil. We play music, light candles, tell stories. And ultimately, we send the person off with a burial or cremation. We remember them, perhaps with a headstone, a small shrine, or a bench in their name. We do these things not for the person we've lost, but to mark the end for ourselves. In order to start feeling better, we have to let the person we loved go.

DREAM UP NOW ⬆

Let's borrow from these ideas and find a way for you to say goodbye to the things you've lost. Think of this as the first small step into the next chapter of your life.

> **Advice I Wish I'd Had**
> "You never really 'get over' a big loss; you just learn to live around the hole it leaves. Not getting over it is okay."
> —Lisa Manterfield

I Feel . . . Peace

Thinking about the questions on this page is a good way to start planning how you might say goodbye to the person or thing you've lost and find peace.

How will you say goodbye? Think about the traditions of burying something or casting it into water. You could bury the letter you wrote in I Feel . . . Loss or something else that is a symbol of the person or thing you've lost—a pet's toy, a college rejection letter, a friend's photograph.

What rituals will you use in your goodbye ceremony? Will you read a poem or the letter you wrote? Light a candle? Play music or dance?

Will you create a physical marker? Maybe you could place an item or a stone in a special place or plant flowers in a corner of a garden. The purpose of a marker is to create a spot where you can go to remember. It could be as simple as sticking a photo on your wall or wearing a special bracelet.

Will you include people in your goodbye ceremony, or would you prefer to be alone? If you want to include other people, make sure they are people who will help you feel better.

When will you say goodbye? Choose a time and place to think about your loss and grief and to say goodbye. Only then can you start to find your way to the next chapter of your life.

Time to say goodbye. Use the space below to fill in any other details about how you will say goodbye to the thing or person you've lost.

Share your art
@dreamupnowjournal
#dreamupnow.

I FEEL . . . JEALOUS

possessiveness / inadequacy / attention-seeking /
critical of self or others / feeling fake

Meet Stacie Shewmake

Stacie struggled with jealousy in high school; comparing herself to others often left her feeling sad. She believed it was hard to separate her own values from the values passed on to her by friends and family. She learned to use music to change her mood. "I don't know if you've tried, but it's impossible to sing when you're sad," she says. "Sometimes I just need to be in my sadness and work up to singing. I'll listen to some of my favorite music and this gets me moving around. When I'm ready to sing, I soon begin feeling better because I'm taking deep breaths, exercising my lungs, getting my heart pumping blood through my veins, and vocalizing loudly. Talk about a release! If I can get to singing, I know I'm doing okay."

Stacie is a board-certified music therapist specializing in music therapy and music lessons for children and teens with special needs. She received her bachelor's degree in music therapy from the University of Minnesota–Twin Cities in 2007, with instrumental emphasis in voice and classical guitar. She resides in Long Beach, California, and practices music therapy in both private and clinical settings, including services for pediatric and NICU at Adventist Health White Memorial Medical Center in East LA and AMUSE Music Center. Learn more about her at expressmusictherapy.com.

Stacie Shares

What is jealousy?

Jealousy is a symptom of feeling insecure in your own self or not appreciating yourself for what you have to offer in your own way. Making others laugh or feel comfortable is a skill, just as much as being able to dance gracefully, paint an interesting portrait, or even keep a tidy room. These all are valuable skills and qualities not everyone possesses.

So maybe you don't have the best fashion sense or you're not that good at math. Not everyone is! First of all, you're not alone. Second, anything you feel you lack you can make up for with something you do well. Make a point to acknowledge your good qualities every day. Write them down. You will find in time that you are adding more and more by the day, and eventually you will be able to be happy for others and celebrate their unique skills rather than feeling like you are in competition with them. Remember, everyone is struggling with something, even if it is not obvious. We all benefit from having more compassion and appreciation for others and what they have to offer in their own special way!

DREAM UP NOW ⬆

Ask yourself:

Who or what are you jealous of?

What do they have that you feel you lack?

Why do you feel you need this? What benefit will it bring you?

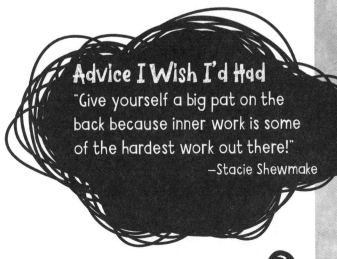

Advice I Wish I'd Had
"Give yourself a big pat on the back because inner work is some of the hardest work out there!"
—Stacie Shewmake

I Feel . . . Jealous

Let's turn around your negative thoughts.

Find a comfortable place where you can listen to music. Now create a playlist of four songs that match the way you are feeling through the lyrics or music. List them here:

Song 1: _____

Artist: _____

Song 2: _____

Artist: _____

Song 3: _____

Artist: _____

Song 4: _____

Artist: _____

How does each song make you feel? Use the space below and on the next page to reflect. Write down any lyrics that match what you are thinking. Write about any past experiences the music reminds you of, or any physical sensations you are feeling (e.g., anxiety, stomach upset, headache).

Next, write words, sensations, and emotions to represent each song. Is there a theme to the words you've written? For example, *pissed off*, *mad*, *annoyed*, *hate*, and *offended* might fall under the umbrella of "angry," but you might feel so strongly about one word or feeling that it deserves its own category.

Choose at least one word per song, but feel free to write more, depending on how strongly you feel or on the ideas and memories the song provokes:

Song 1: _____

_____

Song 2: _____

_____

Song 3: _____

_____

Song 4: _____

_____

Next, for each word you've chosen, write what you think is its opposite (e.g., angry → tolerant, sad → happy, weak → strong, ugly → beautiful).

Song 1: _____

_____

Song 2: _____

_____

Song 3: _____

_____

Song 4: _____

_____

Share your art
@dreamupnowjournal
#dreamupnow.

I FEEL . . . APPRECIATION

being thankful / fueling your positivity for down days /
accepting that "this too shall pass"

Meet Stacie Shewmake

Stacie says, "You are not your thoughts." Your thoughts come and go throughout your day. Some are happy, some sad. Some may be mean, some are kind. She believes that just because you have thoughts that don't make you feel good doesn't mean you can't choose to turn them around. (For more about Stacie, see page 34.)

Stacie describes herself as having "a brain that 'wants' me to suffer." Maybe you can relate. Once she began to observe her thoughts, she realized they were often unkind. The worst part? She believed them. But she soon discovered that these thoughts came from needing unconditional acceptance, understanding, encouragement, and support—things she wasn't getting from the people in her life. So she learned to "parent" herself by turning negative thoughts into positive ones. "It helped me so much," she says.

Stacie Shares

At first it was painful to appreciate and say nice things to myself like, "I am okay with me, no matter what," and "It is okay to feel what I feel."

It took a lot of practice before I began to believe myself, but I kept at it and it really helped. I grew stronger with every kind word I said to myself. The bad thoughts still come and go, but I'm better at choosing kinder ones now. My kindness toward myself makes me feel kinder toward others.

I want to encourage you to choose your own kind thoughts. No one else will ever be able to know what it's like to be you, so be your own best friend.

DREAM UP NOW

Review your positive words from Step 3 in the I Feel . . . Jealous activity. Use those words to create a Positive-Word Playlist of songs you love that represent positive emotions. Search for songs that contain the positive words you wrote. Start by choosing four songs, but don't hold back if you want to add more!

Positive-Word Playlist:

Song 1: _____

Artist: _____

Song 2: _____

Artist: _____

Song 3: _____

Artist: _____

Song 4: _____

Artist: _____

Advice I Wish I'd Had

"You don't need the outside world to validate you when you have a good relationship with yourself. Take a moment each day to appreciate even the smallest things in your life."

—Stacie Shewmake

I Feel . . . Appreciation

As you listen to your new Positive-Word Playlist, write down in the space below everything you're grateful for and appreciate about yourself.

For example, "I'm always on time," or "I'm a really great friend," or "I'm really awesome at _____." You may wish to use words, phrases, or emotions you identify with from your song selections. You can also ask a trusted friend or adult to help.

Read your list of strengths and things you are grateful for out loud a few times, scanning your body as you say these positive words. What do you notice? Do you feel more at ease? Less angry? A little relieved? Review your list and listen to your Positive-Word Playlist any time you need a reminder of how amazing you are. (If you're feeling really bad, go back to the I Feel . . . Jealous activity and do it again. You may have other negative thoughts that need to be turned around—and that's perfectly okay. You can create Positive-Word Playlists to alleviate many emotions.)

Paint, sketch, or make a collage illustrating your list, or use the space on pages 42–43 to write and reflect. Look at your work of art and reflect on it often.

I'm . . .

Share your art
@dreamupnowjournal
#dreamupnow.

CHECK IN

Hey, how are you doing? Go through the list and rate where you feel you are right now. Check back in every once in a while and rate where you are again.

SCALE
1: I need to fix this; 2: Not so great, need help;
3: Meh, could be better; 4: Pretty good; 5: I feel awesome about this

DATE							
I'm a good friend.							
My body feels good, or at least healthy.							
My homework is under control.							
I eat actual vegetables.							
I feel balanced and clearheaded.							
I'm getting enough sleep.							
I do stuff with my family.							

DATE							
Fun is my friend.							
I practice kindness.							
I'm trying to do my best at school.							
I let my creative side out to play.							
I notice when I feel calm.							
I'm done with that one crappy thing.							
I come in contact with nature.							
I exercise for the fun of it.							
I'm pursuing my goals.							

45

I FEEL . . . CONFUSED

forgetful / thoughts that freeze / racing mind /
unable to get stuff done / self-image

Meet Kristin Tollefson

Growing up, Kristin loved drawing, hiking, and exploring in the woods or on the beach in the Pacific Northwest. She spent time with her grandpa working in his woodshop and greenhouse; exploring the collection of old dishes, furniture, and tools that had come from the family farm; and hunting for agates on the beach. She raked smelt (tiny fish she caught in a wire net from the beach), swam in the frigid Puget Sound, sailed, canoed, picked berries, and rode bikes.

Kristin wants to share with you her feelings about dealing with confusion. She says, "I typically take on too many things in life. I often worry about missing out and go way into my head." She discovered that doing something with her hands distracts her from this and makes her feel useful, better.

Kristin has thought of herself as an artist since she was in grade school. She creates sculpture and jewelry, along with public art commissions and installations. She has received several arts fellowships and scholarships, which allowed her to travel as far as Iceland and Chile—four times! Kristin also works as the education director at the Bainbridge Island Museum of Art in Washington state. She's an arts and social justice advocate who speaks out about how art helps people create community and develop a strong sense of self. She believes in the power of firsthand access to art experiences to change lives. Learn more at kltollefson.com and biartmuseum.org.

Kristin Shares

I never felt like I fit in with any particular group—I had lots of friends but struggled with my identity. I was interested in so many things that I didn't align neatly with a specific group of my peers, and I actually liked spending time with my family. Quiet time was important to me, and I think I sometimes came off as being reserved or inaccessible. It was hard for me to find a path through what I thought was a sea of pretty hard-cut choices when I was someone who felt in-between a lot of the time.

When I was 16, I had an opportunity to travel far away from the island where I grew up. I was gone for two months, which gave me a glimpse of people and places beyond my hometown. I had a hard time coming back to a place that felt really small after my world had cracked open. The ridge that lies between childhood and adulthood is so hard to traverse; I wanted the comfort of my family and the home I grew up in, but I wanted to be free and independent. Sometimes those feelings collided, and I found myself in challenging situations.

To calm my busy mind or lay the groundwork for intense creative work, I like to sharpen and arrange my colored pencils. This may not seem like a vastly creative enterprise, but it is therapeutic. Touching the pencils inspires me to think about all the things I can make, and just being around colors is soothing to me. Before I start creating, I can feel a range of emotions from excitement to agitation, but at the end I always feel just . . . *good*. How to find that middle ground, that peaceful place, has been an important piece of information for me. As someone who tends toward drama on my emotional scale, it's so valuable to know that I can self-soothe with this type of organizing activity that preps my mind and hands for something productive.

DREAM UP NOW

Confusion often can come from not having a clearly defined vision for the future. For me, having the opportunity to travel far from home cracked open my world and helped me envision what I wanted from life. Where do you wish you could go, or what do you wish your life could look like, right now? Using the three picture frames on pages 48–49, create images of your past, present, and future. The first frame will show what happened, the second frame is what your life looks like today, and the third frame may be where you want to go, who you want to be, or how you want your life to look. As you complete your three images, notice which one takes the most time.

TIP: They don't have to be completed in order.

Advice I Wish I'd Had
"Some confusion is normal—it ebbs and flows! You already have everything you need inside you. You are enough."
—Kristin Tollefson

I Feel . . . Confused

Grab a pencil, pen, or some colored pencils. You can also cut images out of a magazine or print photos you've taken or images you find online. Now draw or create images of your past, present, and future in the picture frames.

The Past: What Happened

The Present: My Life Right Now

The Future: What I Want

What steps will you need to take to make the third picture come true?

Share your art
@dreamupnowjournal
#dreamupnow.

I FEEL . . . CONFIDENT

gratitude / daring to try something out of your comfort zone / speaking up for yourself

Meet Kristin Tollefson

Kristin hopes you'll experience confidence, clarity, and calm as a result of creating your own Personal Icon. (For more about Kristin, see page 46.) She likes how creating an icon allows your mind to relax, by organizing and letting go at the same time, and to wander its own path. Creating a Personal Icon makes room for you to have emotions that might be tough, like confusion, while channeling your feelings toward a positive outcome.

What is an icon? It's an object or person deserving of devotion; it's an emblem or a symbol. There is no one in the world quite like you. You are building your legacy—who and what you are and will be known for. Creating a Personal Icon can open any number of emotions. Kristin encourages you not to fight your feelings. Instead, allow yourself to accept them, understand them, and, hopefully, find clarity.

Kristin Shares

When I'm feeling solid and confident, I try to take advantage of the strengths I'm embodying to gather my positive energy in a powerful way to make my mark. I have always felt happiest and most confident when I have time and space to create without constraints. Keeping a sketchbook to track ideas (very different from taking photos on my phone!), working with my hands as I think through my thoughts, and making room for failure and exploration have helped me create art. And my art has given me the opportunity to travel to places all over the world—on my own terms. Drawing and sketching have helped me solidify my values and skills and boost my confidence. When I'm confident, I remind myself that I have so much to offer right now, and I bank it for a future time when I might have questions or find myself at a crossroads or on shaky emotional or physical ground. The work you do today while you feel confident will be a useful reminder to you later if you ever experience feelings of confusion or insecurity. Remind yourself of all your strengths.

DREAM UP NOW

I invite you to create a Personal Icon. This project is an easy and fun way to leverage your good feelings today to help you on a "down" day. Grab some old magazines, books, or favorite pics from your phone. We're going to explore your intuition!

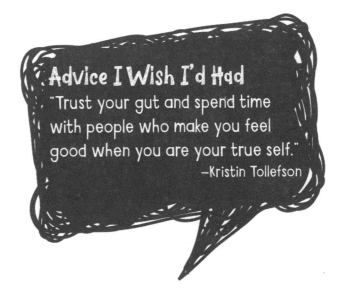

Advice I Wish I'd Had
"Trust your gut and spend time with people who make you feel good when you are your true self."

—Kristin Tollefson

I Feel . . . Confident

To create a Personal Icon, collect magazines, old books, receipts from your wallet, newspaper clippings, photos, or images printed from the internet or your phone. Flip through them at a pace that lets you look at the pictures as you go. Which images make your heart sing? Let your intuition guide your selections. Tear or cut out pictures you like. Don't think too hard about what they are, just make a pile.

When you have roughly 20 images, take a few moments to look through them. Are there themes in what you've chosen? Similarities? Surprises? What strengths, joys, skills, or kind acts describe your best self? Find a pair of scissors and cut out the parts of these pictures that represent your best qualities. Page 53 is your canvas. Start by gluing down one picture, then see where the others need to go. Again, don't think too hard about placement. There's no right or wrong to this activity! You're just making a mark. Know that the images reflect your intuitive self. Look for patterns or themes to help you better understand yourself.

Variation: Find a used deck of playing cards (it does not have to be a complete set). Sometimes you can find a deck for a dollar at a secondhand store. Using one of the cards as your template, draw around some images from your clipping collection. Cut very carefully around the line you've drawn so you can glue each image to the back side of a card. When you are feeling stuck, or less confident than you feel right now, you can sort through the cards in different ways or just look at the images you chose when you felt light and positive.

Share your art
@dreamupnowjournal
#dreamupnow.

I FEEL . . . HURT

emotional pain / powerlessness / replaying agonizing scenario / victimization

Meet Tanesha "Ksyn" Cason

When Tanesha was an adolescent, she had a lot of anger. She didn't know how to let out or handle certain emotions, especially around family issues. She let stuff build up until she felt that if she didn't find a way to let out her hurt feelings, she might take it out on someone. She chose to get her feelings out by dancing. "I would just play a song that was resonating with what I felt and do free movement," she says. Letting out all her feelings through dance, Tanesha would end up feeling so much better, clearer, and ready to take on the day. Being a teen can be tough, especially if you think you're going through everything alone, as Tanesha did. In her senior year of high school, she started taking karate too. It gave her another outlet for working through her feelings.

Tanesha has been acting, modeling, and dancing professionally for over 11 years. She has worked with artists including Usher, Mary J. Blige, Ciara, John Legend, Drake, 50 Cent, Sean Paul, and Beyoncé. Born and raised in New York City, Tanesha graduated from Franklin Pierce University in New Hampshire with a B.S. in arts management with a concentration in dance. She's an advocate for women, teaching positive body awareness and creating a safe environment for women to support each other. You can find her on Instagram @missksyn.

Tanesha Shares

I was mad at so many things when I was a teen. It was just me and my mom. I didn't understand where people were coming from or how to deal with them. In African American culture, it isn't typical to go to therapy. People just push things under the rug. Dancing became my therapy. I would find a safe space to work things out through free movement and dance. Sometimes I used aggressive movements, sometimes soft up-and-down movements. I was like a time bomb. If I didn't dance, I'd take my anger and hurt out on someone. When dancing, though, I could let it all out. Sometimes I would just be crying and dancing.

I had to learn to discipline my mind in addition to dancing. When I found that my mind was cluttered and going in all directions, I could figure things out by freewriting. Getting my feelings out kept them from building up and helped me figure out why I was hurting.

DREAM UP NOW

Try freewriting. No one can explain what you're feeling, because your feelings are your own. Sometimes you have to just get them out and then see what you wrote so you can understand yourself better. Just start with one sentence and go from there. You can try the writing prompt on pages 56–57 or write your own words. None of it has to make sense. Just declutter. It's not an account of your day; it's just exploring all the details of your emotions until they're out of your mind.

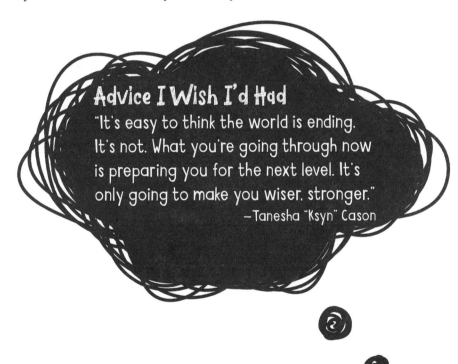

Advice I Wish I'd Had
"It's easy to think the world is ending. It's not. What you're going through now is preparing you for the next level. It's only going to make you wiser, stronger."
—Tanesha "Ksyn" Cason

I Feel . . . Hurt

Today I feel hurt.

If my feelings turned into an animal right now, it would be a

Because

Because

Because

If my feelings turned into an object right now, it would be a

Because

Because

Because

If my feelings turned into a place right now, it would be

Because

Because

Because

Today I feel like

Because

Because

Because

I feel better when I

Because

Because

Because

Share your art
@dreamupnowjournal
#dreamupnow.

I FEEL . . . POWERFUL

confidence / strength / positive self-regard / self-acceptance

Meet Tanesha "Ksyn" Cason

Tanesha believes you can always learn from other people, and you can never know a person's story just by looking at them. (For more about Tanesha, see page 54.) She's traveled the globe, dancing in front of thousands, and yet she struggled with body image as a teen. "It's tempting to pursue an idea of perfection," she says, "but the more important goal is to look at yourself and say: 'What am I happy about with me?' You have to give yourself your own reassurance." In high school, Tanesha surrounded herself with supportive friends in a youth performance group. Performing in the youth group helped improve her self-image because the group represented all different shapes onstage. The priority was for the dancers, models, and actors do their best. "Others will like it or they won't," Tanesha says, "but you need to love yourself, and sometimes that's the hardest part."

Tanesha Shares

From elementary through high school I was very insecure about my body image. When I was 13, I started feeling attracted to boys, but because I was more of a tomboy and was less developed than many of the girls at my school, I wasn't taken seriously. I was teased and bullied about my appearance a lot. People didn't know what I was insecure about, so they brought out my anxiety without knowing it. I tried to laugh it off, but I would get upset and sometimes I would fight or get into arguments. My mouth was kind of reckless.

I joined a youth performing arts group outside of school. That was the beginning of understanding that I wanted to be a professional dancer and performer. Even though I was a tomboy, I began to feel pretty. I had a lot of insecurities, but I still danced, acted, and modeled anyway, to prove to myself that I could do it. I felt more comfortable and like myself when I was performing. So I decided to carry that energy and confidence offstage. I discovered that I could bring the same positive attitude I had when walking in a fashion show or onstage to walking down the street or walking into school.

When I made the whole world my stage, I started to understand myself more. Instead of arrogance or cockiness, I felt appreciation for what I was able to do. I began to believe I wasn't as bad as I thought I was. It helped to know I was good at something.

DREAM UP NOW

When you get older, you start to realize that a lot of the insecurities you had when you were younger may have come from the people in your life. You have to unlearn them and gain body confidence. It's about feeling good about yourself on the inside. Giving yourself affirmations can help.

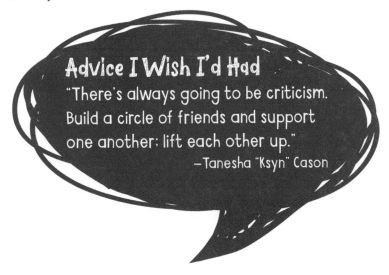

Advice I Wish I'd Had
"There's always going to be criticism. Build a circle of friends and support one another; lift each other up."
—Tanesha "Ksyn" Cason

I Feel . . . Powerful

Visualize what it would look like to carry yourself through your day feeling competent and confident. Sketch a powerful image of yourself.

You can harness feelings of power, confidence, and competence with good posture. Good posture can even improve your focus and brain power and keep your body feeling good. Slouching releases a constant level of excess stress hormones, altering your anxiety levels and mood. Worse, slouching actually cuts oxygen to your brain, damaging your ability to think or concentrate.

Find an empty space with a mirror. Sit or stand in front of it, making the adjustments in the Good Posture Checklist. How do you feel now that your posture conveys that you are powerful and confident?

GOOD POSTURE CHECKLIST

✓ Chin parallel to the floor with eyes up (avoid dipping your chin to look down)

✓ Shoulders level (roll your shoulders up, back, and down)

✓ Arms at your sides (face your wrists forward to naturally open your chest)

✓ Abdominal muscles braced (contract your abs for stability, not your back)

✓ Hips and shoulders even and level

✓ Body weight distributed evenly on both feet

Choose a happy, feel-good song and put it on repeat. From a confident posture, I want you to give yourself affirmations. You can start with the affirmations I'd like you to say (see the table on page 62), but try to write down some personal affirmations too.

1. Begin by staring in the mirror. Rather than picking yourself apart, just look and accept yourself as you are.

2. Tell your reflection the positive affirmations. Stare at yourself in the mirror and smile at yourself as you listen to all your affirmations until you can get to a positive place of acceptance.

3. Ask yourself: *Is there something I want to change?* If you can, change it. If you can't, accept it.

4. Begin to move, dance. Move freely, crazily—it doesn't matter.
   (I do this every day!)

5. Post your favorite affirmations on the mirror and read them every day.

Try to do this every morning for 15 minutes to start the day in a powerful place.

TANESHA WANTS ME TO SAY TO MYSELF:	MY PERSONAL AFFIRMATIONS:
I am beautiful.	
I am amazing.	
I'm still growing.	
I'm still learning.	
I am powerful.	
I'm okay with me.	
I'm in control.	
I'm awesome just as I am.	
This is me. If people love it, okay. If they don't, that's okay too.	

I FEEL . . . LONELY

worrying / friends & friendship / isolation /
longing for closeness / dealing with suicide & heartbreak

Meet Korum Bischoff

Korum is a cheerful and talented guy who has a wide circle of friends. Most people would never guess he's suffered the devastating shock of the suicides of several loved ones. "My best friend committed suicide four years ago," he says. "Other super important people to me have taken their own lives too." If you've also faced the loneliness that comes from loss, you may recognize the temptation go within, to shut down. Korum challenges you to widen your circle of friends instead. "Find people who lift you up, share your interests, and make life a more enjoyable and fulfilling journey." Sometimes amazing people are found where we least expect them, and Korum hopes you will look beyond your current circle to find common ground in other groups and relief from loneliness.

Korum is a Grammy-nominated drummer and songwriter who has recorded six albums with the band Recess Monkey. Korum began drumming at 10 years old and has worked as a professional drummer for 20 years. He has worked with several bands, recording over 20 albums throughout his career. He also interacts with artists and their art every day as a marketing director for an art museum. Learn more at korumdrum.com.

Korum Shares

I have a problem with obsessing with thoughts. I remember a long drive where all I could think about was the word *Mississippi*. I just kept thinking about how it looks, how it's spelled, how it sounds. But sometimes I obsess about less trite thoughts, like about my uncle who committed suicide in my grandma's house and what the room looked like afterward. I get so angry at him for ruining my grandma's house. It was the one place that was a constant for me, a sanctuary.

As a drummer, music is my refuge when I'm feeling overwhelmed and alone in the world. I put on some music that matches the feelings I'm going through and just pound it all out on my drums. Drumming takes my mind off whatever I'm thinking about. While playing, I can let my mind focus on something else. It's the physical act—like running, or lifting weights, or hitting a punching bag. For me, drumming accomplishes the same thing. I play until I get tired, but I end up feeling restored.

DREAM UP NOW

The only time I can open up to other social groups is when I make a solid decision to do so. If I go in with a thought like, "I'm not going to like this," I find I'm unable to open myself. I often fall prey to stereotypes. But by intentionally checking my stereotypes and bias, I can give new situations and people a chance. I can start to see the other person's point of view and allow myself to connect. I like to meet all kinds of people, especially people whose interests, backgrounds, or lives look very different from my own. Growing up in a polarized world, I didn't know anything else beyond my back door, so I am always trying to open myself and become more tolerant and curious. I want to help you connect too.

Advice I Wish I'd Had
"We should always have three friends in our lives. One who walks ahead who we look up to and follow; one who walks beside us, who is with us every step of the journey; and one who we reach back for and bring along once we've cleared the way."
—Michelle Obama

I Feel . . . Lonely

One of the first steps to relieving loneliness is recognizing that others might be struggling with similar problems. A profound way teens around the world express and experience their feelings is through music. Let's try expanding your world using my 3-3-3 Method. You'll need access to a streaming music service to begin.

First, list three things you feel right now. (Ideas: alone, lonely, depressed, stressed, worried, outcast, misunderstood, hurt, overwhelmed, lost, out of control, jealous, numb, bored, bad, tired)

1._____

2._____

3._____

Next, find three songs in an unfamiliar music genre that match your feelings. The three words you chose above are your search keywords. Open your streaming music and begin searching for songs or lyrics with your words. You may find some great songs already in your playlist. But I want you to do something different today: go way out beyond your comfort zone and search for songs from artists you've never listened to or in a style you've never explored. You may have to seek out translations of lyrics in unfamiliar languages. Be open.

Here are some genres to consider: alternative, Americana, blues, Christian and gospel, classic rock, classical, country, dance, electronic, experimental, hard rock, hip-hop, indie, jazz, K-pop, Latino, metal, Música Mexicana, Música Tropical, oldies, pop, pop Latino, rap, R&B, reggae, rock, rock y alternativo, soul/funk, showtunes, world music.

My newfound three songs:

Song 1:_____

Artist: _____

Song 2:_____

Artist: _____

Song 3:_____

Artist: _____

Last, listen to each song you found three times. Allow your newfound music to speak to what you're going through. Allow it to resonate with your heart.

It can be comforting to discover that someone you've never met, in some faraway place, has put words to what you feel. Sometimes, songs without words can offer the perfect soundtrack to your emotions too. It's okay to be lonely right now. Please know you are not alone. Someone, somewhere, felt lonely enough to share his/her/their music with you.

Use the space below to write or draw about how you feel when listening to your newfound music. If you need help now, I encourage you to talk to someone you trust, or reach out to one of the hotlines or apps in the resources section of this journal.

What I Feel When Listening to My Newfound Music

Share your art
@dreamupnowjournal
#dreamupnow.

I FEEL . . . SOCIABLE

building a positive circle of friends / pursuing your interests /
speaking up for what you want

Meet Korum Bischoff

Korum knows how hard it can be to figure out where you fit in. He struggled with that too, even though he had a variety of interests. (For more about Korum, see page 63.) "It felt good to be a bit of a chameleon," he says, "but sometimes I felt like I didn't have a home base." In high school he hung out with artists, drama kids, athletes, band members, and religious kids, but never gave 100 percent to any one group. He found himself at varying skill levels in each area. He remembers, "I didn't feel like I had a group of people. I didn't ever feel like I had super deep connections in any of those groups." So, how do you accept where you are and find your tribe? Korum wants to show you how to start—by setting a goal for where you want to be and understanding that we're all at different stages.

Korum Shares

I had a friend who was a good artist in high school. I had always enjoyed drawing too. One time we drove around with sketch pads, and whenever we found something that struck us, we'd stop, get out of the car, and sketch it. I'm not a good artist. I had to let go of the fact that my friend was better at it and just enjoy doing art with him, even if all we were sketching was a mailbox. I told myself, "You're not competing to get into a gallery, just enjoying something that you both like doing." That day, I discovered that I could feel accepted even if my work wasn't as good as his. I found that I felt comfortable with him. I had to have faith in myself and decide to trust another person.

It isn't easy. I've drummed for 30 years and have been nominated for a Grammy, and I still get intimidated by other musicians—even my own brother. He's recorded and performed with legendary artists, and while those performers are not in the room when we're together, I can still feel the pressure of his success.

How do you accept yourself for not being as good as you want to be? It helps to remember that no matter who is in your group, everyone is trying to get better. You may think someone is already there, that they've reached the highest level. But while you think this person already is the best, they probably don't feel that way. There is always room for improvement. Everyone wants to be better, learn more, achieve more. We can get so caught up in our own process that we forget that the other person is on their own journey as well—and might even need *our* help. My friend the painter, he just wanted to get out and sketch. But he didn't have the nerve to stop in front of someone's mailbox by himself and draw it. He needed me at his side.

There was a guy in my high school who carried drumsticks everywhere and was always drumming on everything. He got voted "Most Musical." He really was just practicing all the time because he wasn't at the level he wanted to reach. But everyone else perceived him as being a great drummer. You need to trust that people are going to accept you, even if you think you're not as good.

DREAM UP NOW

What is it you like to do, and how do you get together with other people? I'll tell you how to make a plan for connecting with people who do the things you like to do.

Advice I Wish I'd Had
"Don't let people scare and shame you into changing the things about yourself that make you unique and interesting. Those are the qualities that will make your life so magical."
—Kesha

I Feel . . . Sociable

How can you build up the courage to ask others to do your favorite activities with you, whether it's playing guitar, going to a yoga class, working out at the gym, or acting? Let's make a plan to connect.

What are some things you'd like to do? Figure out your goal. For example, "I want to learn how to cook," or "I want to try out for the school play," or "I want to be in a band/draw better/do photography." Whatever it is, write it down.

I want to _____.

Now, write down the names of three people you know and respect who do what you love or want to do:

1._____

2._____

3._____

Approaching these people might feel intimidating, but knowing what to say can help you feel prepared. Begin by making a statement in your mind about where you are, honestly, and where you'd like to be (your goal).

My current skill level: _____.

My goal: _____.

Find a time to approach each person you mentioned. Say what you see. For example: "I see you are always carrying your guitar around/making great drawings/posting

awesome pictures online/_____."

Then, be honest. "I'm interested in _____ too,

and I've always wanted to _____.

Then, acknowledge where you are: _____

_____

_____.

(For example: "I want to play with other people, but I only play guitar at home by myself." Or, "I really want to start going to the gym, but I don't know what to do and don't want to look stupid.")

Be brave. Ask for what you really want: "I was wondering if sometime we could hang out when you're going to do _____."

If the response is yes, be ready to make a specific plan for when: "I'll talk to you tomorrow at lunch and we'll figure out a time that works." If that person declines, let it go. You were honest with them, so be thankful for this person's honesty too. If one person is not able to share their interests, find another who will. You don't want to waste your time. Surround yourself with positive, open people who encourage one another. If circumstances change, that person who said no may come to you later when they're ready. Remember, everyone is on his/her/their own journey.

Share your art
@dreamupnowjournal
#dreamupnow.

I FEEL . . . PERFECTIONISM

insecurity / unreasonable demands on self / comparison with others

Meet Shelley Klammer

As a teen, Shelley struggled with being afraid that people would not like who she really was. Trying to fit into outside standards, she often felt the pain of changing herself to please other people. She learned that the fear of not being accepted can cause you to cover up your authentic self by wearing a social mask. She says, "Wearing a social mask creates distance between you and other people, so you feel alone even as you are trying to belong."

Because you feel pressure to appear perfect for other people, you might think that you're the only one who is secretly struggling with feeling not good enough. In Shelley's work as a counselor, she sees that, actually, most people do not feel worthy when they are trying to measure up to outside standards.

Shelley created Expressive Art Workshops, where she facilitates emotional healing through expressive art and writing. A former teen model and beauty pageant contestant, she is now a counselor and expressive arts educator. Learn more about Shelley and check out her online art programs at expressiveartworkshops.com.

Shelley Shares

As a teen, I worried a lot about what other people thought about me. I changed myself like a chameleon to fit into every party. I remember practicing my best smile in the mirror before I went out. Instead of focusing on what I loved about myself, I was always trying to figure out what others thought of me.

I was a perfectionist, and I competed in pageants as a teen model. In the modeling business, I was judged more by my outer appearance than my inner intelligence. I struggled with an eating disorder in an effort to stay perfectly thin. I felt like I had two selves. I had a true self that I hid in my journals, and I had an outer self that tried to please others.

In my journals, I secretly explored my creative visions. I was a big dreamer as a teen, and I had 22 different careers picked out for my future. I wanted to be a writer, a fashion designer, a photographer, a jewelry maker, a gallery artist . . . the list went on and on.

Finally, I settled into what I love to do. I teach people how to share their emotions through expressive art and writing. This is because I have created art every day since I was a teen, and it has helped me express my authentic self in the world.

DREAM UP NOW ↑

Taking a look at the "outside face" you present to the world and the "inside face" that expresses who you authentically are increases self-awareness and self-acceptance. In this activity and the activity for I Feel . . . Worthy, you will look at the contrast between these two faces.

Advice I Wish I'd Had
"Express your uniqueness and you will find your true life direction."
—Shelley Klammer

I Feel . . . Perfectionism

The purpose of this exercise is to create a piece of art that represents the "perfect" face that you show the outside world to try to fit in—your social mask. The face you choose will be decorated with words and images that show how you present yourself to others.

Choose a face from a magazine that represents perfection for you. Also look for another face that represents your authentic self. (You will need to have two faces to alter and expressively draw on for this activity and the next one. Set aside the face representing your authentic self for now.)

If you prefer to create your own face, draw an oval. Then draw eyes, a nose, and a mouth inside the oval.

Altered Magazine Photo I—Perfectionism

What you'll need:

magazines; scissors; a glue stick; permanent black, colored, and white markers for doodling and coloring (permanent markers work best for altering magazine photos)

What you'll do:

1. Cut out the face you chose that represents perfection and glue it onto page 74.

2. This "outside face" is the perfect face you show to others. Consider all the ways you try to gain approval from others as you work on altering this face.

3. Expressively draw and color on your face in any way you like. Add patterns, words, and symbols to represent what your public self looks like to the outside world.

4. **Suggestions:** Glue your magazine face on page 74. Glue on other magazine images and words to illustrate your theme. Outline and draw over and around your magazine collage with a black permanent marker. Color your doodles. Embellish your altered drawing with a white paint marker or gel pens.

Share your art
@dreamupnowjournal
#dreamupnow.

I FEEL . . . WORTHY

self-acceptance / positive self-image / courage / self-respect / honor

Meet Shelley Klammer

Years before she learned about how art can heal emotions, Shelley was a secret journal writer who loved to draw. (For more about Shelley, see page 71.) In her teens, Shelley believed her inside self did not match her outside self. Drawing and writing in her journals provided a place for her to practice being totally authentic. As she built up more courage in her journals, she began sharing more of her authentic self with the outer world. "Nobody is perfect," she says, "and trying to please everybody is exhausting. It takes a lot of energy to pretend to be someone you are not. You can't relax when you are constantly second-guessing your thoughts and actions."

Shelley Shares

I was bullied by a group of girls when I was 14 years old. After that, I felt afraid to express my uniqueness. In high school, I thought it would be safer to generalize myself and match whoever I was with. I became very popular. I fit into every group and I was invited to lots of parties, yet I felt like I was no one. Even though it appeared as if I had many "friends," I felt unworthy of the attention. Now I know that our differences are needed to help heal our world. The things that make you special and unique point to your authentic self. And your authenticity informs your true life direction. Questions you might ask when you reflect upon your unique purpose are *Who am I? Where do I belong? When do I feel fulfilled?*

DREAM UP NOW

Before others can genuinely appreciate you, you need to appreciate yourself. Accepting yourself and others makes it easier to take off your social mask. Be sure to notice how you judge others. When you focus on the negative qualities in other people, you will also focus more on your own negative qualities.

Pick one thing each day that you disapprove of about yourself and find a way to approve of it. Practicing daily self-approval will, over time, turn into genuine self-love.

Create a list of your unique qualities. Close your eyes and consider who you genuinely are. Write a list of all the good things that make you authentically *you*. They might not be things that everyone in your life admires. There will be some things that only you recognize and like about yourself.

Things I Like About Myself:

_____   _____

_____   _____

_____   _____

Choose a good quality from your list and speak to yourself about it in a kind and approving way for an entire day.

Three Ways to Speak Kindly to Yourself

If you care too much about what other people think, it can be challenging to accept positive affirmations from the first-person perspective. Talking to yourself in ways that others might talk to (or about) you taps into the social part of your brain. Saying kind words in a second- or third-person perspective helps you powerfully anchor the calm safety of social approval.

First-person perspective: I am _____.
(good, kind, funny, smart, etc.)

Second-person perspective: (Your name)_____,

you are _____.

Third-person perspective: He/she/they is/are

_____.

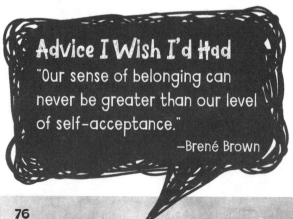

Advice I Wish I'd Had
"Our sense of belonging can never be greater than our level of self-acceptance."

—Brené Brown

I Feel . . . Worthy

Create a drawing that represents the authentic face you express when you feel safe or when you are alone. The face you choose will be decorated with words and images that show how you genuinely feel on the inside. Your "inside face" expresses who you authentically are. This activity can help you increase self-awareness and self-acceptance.

Use the second clipped-out magazine face you set aside in the I Feel . . . Perfectionism activity. Or, if you prefer to create your own face, simply draw an oval. Then add eyes, a nose, and a mouth inside the oval.

Altered Magazine Photo II—Self-Worth

What you'll need:

magazines, scissors, a glue stick, permanent black, colored, and white markers for doodling and coloring (permanent markers work best for altering magazine photos)

What you'll do:

1. Cut out the face you chose that represents your authentic self and glue it onto page 78.

2. This "inside face" will be about the private face you do not yet show to others. Consider these questions as you draw: *Who am I? Where do I belong? When do I feel fulfilled?*

3. Expressively draw and color your face in any way you like. Add patterns, words, and symbols to represent what your private self looks like to your inside world.

4. **Suggestions:** Glue your magazine face on page 78. Glue on other magazine images and words to illustrate your theme. Outline and draw over and around your magazine collage with a black permanent marker. Color your doodles. Embellish your altered drawing with a white paint marker or gel pens.

Share your art
@dreamupnowjournal
#dreamupnow.

I FEEL . . . SAD

failure / depression or despair / powerlessness / vulnerability / sense of lack

Meet Rich Redmond

If Rich is having a bad day, he says playing the drums resets his emotional and physical spirit. "Nothing good can happen when you're holding onto sadness," he says. "If I'm tired, if I'm sick, if I feel depressed, I still have to go out and drum. The audience is expecting the rhythmic energy of the band, the band is relying on me to set the rhythm, and ultimately playing music is good for me. I'll be healed." Problems don't disappear when Rich commits to pursuing the thing he loves, but his sadness is replaced by happiness, and everything is better for a while. "Drumming is my medicine," he says. Think about activities you enjoy that help you get back on track and create positivity. If there's something that brings *you* joy, Rich encourages you to do it.

Rich has been a pro drummer for 30 years, and he also works as an actor, a speaker, a producer, and an author. Rich earned his master's degree in music education and is an adjunct professor at the University of North Alabama. Rich has recorded 23 #1 singles and plays to sold-out crowds in arenas and stadiums around the world. *Modern Drummer* magazine voted Rich Country Drummer of the Year in 2015 and 2016, and he was voted Best Country Drummer by *Drum!* in 2011. When not on the road, he splits his time between Nashville, Tennessee, and Los Angeles, California. Learn more at richredmond.com and youtube.com /richredmond.

Rich Shares

When you're feeling sad, it can help to think about all the things you're thankful for. There are people right now who don't have access to clean drinking water. I do. Every morning in the shower, I make a list of everything I'm grateful for. Sometimes it's silly, I admit. And sometimes I just say, "I'm really happy for my health, my family, my friends."

It doesn't have to be anything big or impress anyone else. I might say, "Thank you for introducing me to Taylor, who introduced me to Alex, who has become a trusted friend."

Sometimes I go big: "Thank you for my talent that lets me live my life and do something that makes a difference and also makes me happy."

I just go down the list of things I'm personally super happy about and then I start the day appreciating that I have a killer life.

You choose happiness. When you step out of bed every morning, you can choose how you feel about your situation. For example, I can complain: "I'm so sick of being lactose intolerant." Or, I can say to myself: "Dude, this is going to be such a great day. I'm going to put extra coconut milk in my iced coffee." Gratitude is a great antidote for staying out of the negative. I intentionally choose to be positive and stay positive. Every time I have a sandwich, I stop and think, "Wow, I really like how these flavors are coming together. This bread is really good." I'm in the business of happiness. If I could, I'd sell happiness door to door.

You've probably heard how habits are formed by repetition. This includes your thoughts. If your thoughts are persistently negative, you're going to feel negative. By thinking positive thoughts, you choose happiness. Life is a collection of experiences, and if you live in the moment and try to make each day as happy as possible, you can string those happy days together and look back and think, "Wow, I have a pretty good life."

DREAM UP NOW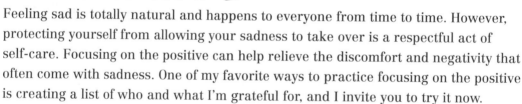

Feeling sad is totally natural and happens to everyone from time to time. However, protecting yourself from allowing your sadness to take over is a respectful act of self-care. Focusing on the positive can help relieve the discomfort and negativity that often come with sadness. One of my favorite ways to practice focusing on the positive is creating a list of who and what I'm grateful for, and I invite you to try it now.

Advice I Wish I'd Had
"We are what we repeatedly do."
—Aristotle

I Feel . . . Sad

When you're feeling sad, it can help to think about all the things you're thankful for. Identify the things that give you joy in life. Remember some things you were worried about when you were feeling negative and how maybe they didn't turn out to be so bad. Start small and then go bigger.

I'm wearing some cool shoes. ⟶ **I go to a good school.**

I have clothes to wear. ⟶ **I like my mom's new boyfriend.**

Who are you thanking? That's up to you. Who you thank is as personal as your gratitude list. You may be thanking yourself, you may be thanking the universe, or you may be thanking your higher power. I trust you to know your path.

If you need more help or would like someone to talk to about your sadness, reach out to a hotline or app listed in the resource section at the end of this journal.

Share your art
@dreamupnowjournal
#dreamupnow.

I FEEL . . . HAPPY

positive self-regard / friends & friendship / giving to others / gratitude

Meet Rich Redmond

Each piece of the drum kit is an individual instrument, uniquely crafted and perfected to create its own sound. The high hat is not expected to behave like the kick drum. Each piece can be played alone, but when played together like movements in a symphony, they create an entirely new experience. Assembled, the individual pieces become an entirely new instrument. As a professional drummer, Rich Redmond is the support system of the band, its backbone and keeper of the rhythm, laying the foundation for the other instruments to play their own songs. (For more about Rich, see page 79.) If those musicians are to be successful, the drummer must first be successful. There is great sense of belonging, of being an essential part of the whole, without the need to be the front person.

Rich Shares

Focusing on something you love can lead to a lot of happiness.

All I wanted was a sense of belonging when I was in high school. I was never in the cool kids' club, but I was lucky that I'd found my thing.

Drumming gave me purpose, kept me focused. I made a commitment to be a professional drummer in 1982 when the Police's *Synchronicity* came out. I found my social clique in jazz band and marching band. Playing in band helped me become a focused kid, and focus is the opposite of chaos. I didn't know then what my career would look like or how long it would take to get there, but playing music in a group gave me a sense of belonging.

One of the first things I teach my drum students is Alone and Together, a drumming technique that involves doing four things at once. If I find myself slipping from my happy place, I surround myself with friends, and we are alone, together. We might listen to great music, eat delicious food, or watch a favorite movie. The good feelings come from being part of the whole.

The thing about drumming is that it's a supportive instrument. Really everything I do in life is about making other people comfortable. Music, and drumming in particular, is a service industry. Drummers support a song, we support an artist, we support a band, we support a record label, we support a producer. We're literally there to make all these people's jobs easier. Playing in bands gave me a sense of teamwork early on and taught me how to take direction from people. I came to realize that, in general, taking direction is how we get through life. It's how successful people rise to the top: the ability to take direction without being offended.

DREAM UP NOW

To find, celebrate, and maintain your good feelings of happiness, think about the groups you belong to and how you support them. Your part in the group brings everyone else happiness too.

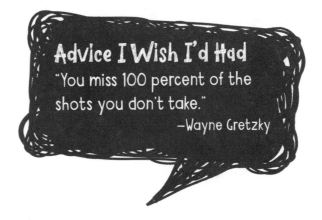

Advice I Wish I'd Had
"You miss 100 percent of the shots you don't take."
—Wayne Gretzky

I Feel . . . Happy

Find some colored pencils or pens. See the stage on page 85? Imagine that you are standing on this stage. Draw a figure that represents you or glue in a picture of yourself. The audience is everyone and everything in your world: your family, friends, part-time job, after-school activity—anyone or anything that is significant to you right now.

Happiness is a function of sharing yourself. How do you lift up, inspire, or support others?

Color in beams of light, shining from you on the stage out to these individuals and groups in the audience. In each beam of light, add a few words about how you share your abilities or help that person or group in some way. Take this time to acknowledge that you, the performer, are needed, skilled, giving, and important in the world of everyone in your audience. You are someone else's safe place and shining light.

Feel like you could do more? List three things you can do to share more of yourself or improve the success of your groups, family, and circle of friends. Every time you are successful, everyone else is successful too, because you're contributing to the whole. The same is true for everyone in your audience; their individual successes support and lift you up in return!

Three things I can do to give more of myself to the important people in my life:

Share your art
@dreamupnowjournal
#dreamupnow.

I FEEL . . . CYNICISM

feeling held back / judging others & being judged / negative group-thought

Meet André Hardy

André defines cynicism as buying into group-thought or stereotypes and having a fixed mind-set. He believes you can own your destiny, your future, by "voiding" cynicism. Rather than perpetuating cynicism, he encourages you to crush it. The cynical thought André grew up around was, "If you look like this, you belong here. If you look like that, this is going to happen to you." André never believed that about himself. "I really dug football," he says. "I said I wanted to be pro. People told me, 'You don't know how, you don't play, you haven't been coached. It's never going to happen.'" The cynicism didn't affect him because he focused on three rewards that were more important than anyone's doubt: "1) I really enjoy the game, 2) I recognized I could go to college for free, and 3) I wanted to make a living at it," he explains. What does cynicism look like in your world?

André is a former NFL running back who was the only black man in his Master of Fine Arts writing program at Antioch University in Los Angeles. André began writing in 2005 and is at work on a hard-boiled detective novel. He's the author of independent essays, creative nonfiction, noir and mystery fiction, and critical analysis, and is an author-interviewer for the *Los Angeles Review of Books*. André was drafted by the Philadelphia Eagles in 1984. He then went on to play for the San Francisco 49ers and the Seattle Seahawks until he retired in 1988. Learn more at andrehardy.net.

André Shares

As a black male growing up in an urban environment with no fathers, I was cynical about life in general—cynicism was built into my community. The mindset was that you were predestined to a certain station. Most of the people around me thought there were only a limited number of opportunities and there was a game to play—with very little possibility of winning.

I never believed that applied to me. I don't think like that.

There are statistics you can buy into, maybe about the likelihood of ending up in jail, along with the belief that there's not a lot you can do about them. This cynicism comes from group-thought, the beliefs of the people in your immediate world. If you're in a community where people expect that you'll never graduate from high school, you can choose to resign yourself to that. Or, you can void it by turning the group-thought on its head: you *will* graduate, you *will* become something. If you break barriers and buck trends, you are voiding cynicism.

Advice I Wish I'd Had

"There will always be situations that can't be controlled. But we always have control over our response. Peace comes from knowing that life is made up of events of which we ultimately decide the meaning."

—André Hardy

When you know the answers in class but hold back your intellect because you don't want to look uncool, you are buying into group-thought. But if you want to be successful, you do your homework, study, go to college. You void cynicism when you say, "I don't agree with the group," and let go of the idea that life is static—that it won't change or get any better. Finding the courage to step out and try to achieve your dreams requires you to deal with cynicism.

If you're the cynical one holding others to group-thought, get in touch with what moves you and inspires you: art, writing, sports, music, performing, playing chess, video games—whatever you have an intimate connection with that excites you. If you nurture your connection with the thing you love, you'll discover a willingness to defeat cynicism and gain the personal rewards that come with pursuing your passion. To get there, you have to stay on the road of nurturing your passion. You have to focus on the end result and not let go of it. Even if you can't see the whole road ahead of you, just stay on it with the end dream in mind. You don't know how long that road is going to be, but there will be milestones and successes along the way that indicate your progress and show that you're getting closer. Enjoy them.

DREAM UP NOW ⬆

To achieve your dreams and goals in life, you have to challenge cynicism and group-thought. More importantly, you have to take some time to reflect on what you believe. Use the table on pages 88–89 to identify what the people in your life think about each issue, and then search your heart and mind to determine what you believe as an individual. Your beliefs may be very different from those of the people closest to you, and that's okay.

I Feel . . . Cynicism

In the table below, identify your beliefs and expectations and how cynical group-thought might be affecting your hopes and dreams.

ISSUE	GROUP-THOUGHT	WHAT I BELIEVE
Spirituality/Religion		
School/Intellect		
Family		
Friendships		
Social Media		
Political Issues		
Mental Health		
Money		

ISSUE	GROUP-THOUGHT	WHAT I BELIEVE
Food/Lifestyle		
Love/Relationships		
Drugs/Alcohol/ Substance Use		
Gender		
Weight/Body Image		
Jobs/Employment		
Other		
Other		
Other		
Other		

What is my passion?

What do I want for my future?

How is my dream for my life similar to or different from the group-thought?

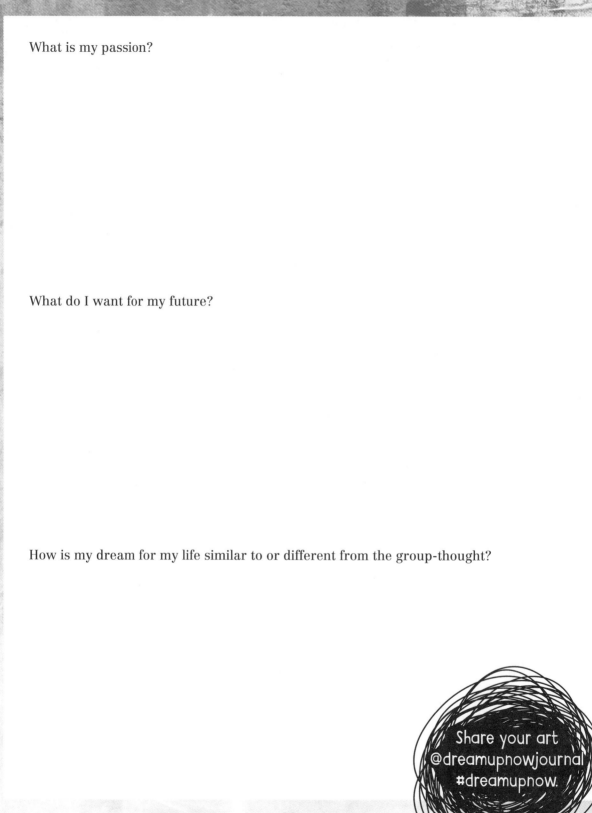

Share your art
@dreamupnowjournal
#dreamupnow.

I FEEL . . . FAITH

trusting yourself / taking steps to pursue your goals /
patience / honesty & authenticity

Meet André Hardy

André recognizes that the world is changing every minute. How are you still standing? He believes that this strength comes from passion and wants to know, *What are you passionate about? What can your passion bloom into?* "I am in love with art," he says, and he continues to set new goals for his art. (For more about André, see page 86.) "On the road to your dream, there will be bumps and bruises. Faith is about staying on that road." André points out that if you're a person who feels high school seems pointless, it's important to find a connection to what is next after graduation. If you make a plan for the future, you'll have something to work toward. It can be scary and it can be tough, so André recommends finding a mentor, an adult you can trust who will take that walk of faith with you.

André Shares

For me, faith has always been about focusing on my goal and reaffirming the things I love. It helps me get out of bed each day. It doesn't matter how big or far-reaching a goal you set for yourself is. If you take small bites, you can eat a whole elephant. Faith, for me, is doing. It's not anything spiritual; it is very practical. Faith is a driver. If I do a certain thing, there's an outcome. If you cut your arm, you'll bleed. If you practice the piano, you'll become a better pianist.

The loss of faith is failing to identify the thing you're passionate about. If you don't know your goal, you can't know the process to achieve it.

Faith is knowing what moves you and finding the process—the training, the study, the immediate steps—that will move you toward your goal. Between the thing you love and the end result is faith.

If you got in your car and said, "I want to drive to Disneyland," but didn't set your GPS to get there, there's no telling where you'd end up. You might get to Disneyland, sure, but it's not likely. However, if you establish a path to get there, even though you might have to stop to buy gas, fix a flat tire, eat lunch, or resolve an unexpected problem, you will reach your destination. And you'll enjoy the sights along the way. Don't put your head down, and don't ignore the milestones.

You'll also find it is smoother, and probably a lot more interesting, if the person behind the wheel already knows the way and can show it to you. When I was a teen dreaming of playing in the NFL, it was easy for me to see football players on TV modeling what I wanted. Find a mentor who is doing what you love and listen to them, learn from them.

DREAM UP NOW ⬆

If you want to play tennis, design games, produce music, sing, become a doctor, whatever your end goal, it is easier if you have the help of a mentor who has already walked the path you're about to take.

Maybe you're curious about computer design or programming, for instance. Companies are interested in the next generation of talent, and for a practical reason: recruitment. A young person who exhibits the desire to reach out and learn appears highly motivated. Seek out your mentor.

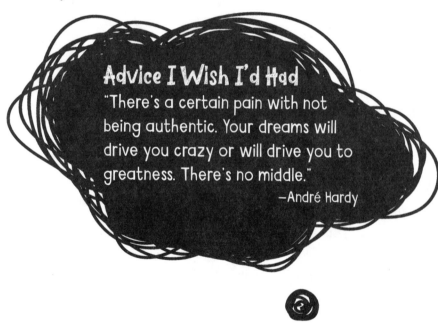

Advice I Wish I'd Had
"There's a certain pain with not being authentic. Your dreams will drive you crazy or will drive you to greatness. There's no middle."
—André Hardy

I Feel . . . Faith

Is there someone in your community who is doing something you admire? Reach out. Make a list of 10 people, companies, or organizations you would like to spend a day with, learning about their careers and responsibilities.

Ten mentors who have the title, position, or experience I dream of achieving:

POTENTIAL MENTOR	NOTES

Not sure how to contact the 10 people on your list? Ask yourself: *Why is this mentorship important to me?* And then share that with your potential mentors. Consider calling to set up an appointment to meet for five minutes if your mentor is local, or send an email to introduce yourself. You might say:

I'm really interested in _____. (Personalize it!)

Tell your potential mentor:

 1. Exactly what you want:

 2. Why you value them as a mentor:

 3. What you hope to get out of the mentorship:

Be sure to consider the above three questions for each person on your list. Use your answers to create a script or email template to use when reaching out.

Trust your instincts; as a teen, you have a great bull-crap meter. You often can tell a lot about a person from speaking with them. A good mentor sees you for your talents and abilities and doesn't try to live their life through you or get you to do something they weren't able to do. When you've chosen a trustworthy adult as your mentor, share your dream, even if it's not yet clearly defined. Working together to pursue your goal will stoke your passion and fire you up. If a teen said to me, "Hey, I'm an aspiring writer. Can you help me? I know you write hard-boiled detective fiction, and I want to learn from you," I'd say, "Absolutely, yes."

If someone says no to mentoring you, remember this: *rejections are rarely personal.* A rejection doesn't say anything about you as a person. This adult may be too busy, they may already have a mentee, or they may doubt their ability to be a quality mentor. Some of the people on your list may not even reply. That's normal. If a business sends out an advertisement, it might get a 1 percent return. Don't be upset if you don't get 100 percent positive responses. It has nothing to do with you. As a writer, I can tell you that rejections are a badge of honor. It means you're in it. It means you actually tried. Part of the road is bumps and bruises.

ANGRY RANT

What makes you mad? Like seething, blind-rage mad? What can you not stand? What would you never accept, not for a bazillion dollars? What is wrong with this world? Rant it!

Share your art
@dreamupnowjournal
#dreamupnow.

I FEEL . . . ANXIOUS

vulnerability / shame / powerlessness /
sensitivity / worrying about outcomes

Meet Rayne Lacko

As a teen, Rayne dealt with anxiety by escaping into a daydream life, creating made-up characters who lived dramatic and romantic lives of creativity and confidence, unlike her own in small-town Canada. A common trigger of anxiety is having to commit to one potential interest or path while giving up other equally tempting choices. Unsure of what the future held for her, Rayne studied liberal arts in college to feed her many passions: reading books, discussing music and philosophy, writing, and studying languages. She longed to travel to the faraway places she read about and immerse herself in the languages she floundered with in textbooks. From college into adulthood, she traveled, always seeking a place to call home. She now lives happily on a forested island with her husband, children, dog, and cat.

Rayne believes music, language, and art connect us, and she explores those themes in her books, *A Song for the Road* and *Dream Up Now*. Rayne grew up in Canada, earning a liberal arts degree in Toronto, including a semester in Spain, and a graphic design diploma in Vancouver. She migrated to the West Coast to San Diego and Orange County, California, where she attended UCLA's writer's program. She now resides in the Pacific Northwest, where she is secretary on the board of trustees at a performing arts organization. She cohosts a library youth writing workshop and an annual filled-to-capacity writing camp, and she established Teen Creatives Live, a twice-annual open mic event for teens. For over a decade, Rayne edited an outdoor adventure magazine. Learn more at raynelacko.com.

Rayne Shares

Anxiety looks different for everyone. Growing up, I was terrified of revealing my inner world. Some people choose to hide the workings of their hearts by keeping to themselves, becoming stoic and cold, and that makes sense. Me? I became a writer. My entire career objective is to reveal the scenes playing out in my head—and make them compelling for others.

Another anxiety trigger for me is public speaking. Ironically, I choose to teach creative writing to teens, and even helped establish Teen Creatives Live, an open mic event. It may seem like I'm weirdly into self-torture, but I'm so passionate about writing (and writers) that I've learned to accept that I'll be anxious and just do scary things like public speaking anyway.

What triggers your anxiety? Big tests and exams? Important athletic competitions? Dating? Your anxiety is tied to the emotions you have about the thing that worries you. The more important the thing is (for me, it's writing and teaching), the more emotions you'll have about it.

Some would say I'm "too sensitive." I cry during movies or books when the characters find hope after despair or realize a bitter and painful truth and grow stronger from it. My emotional reactions to events (even fictional ones) are very real. I have to avoid horror movies and situations with terror or abuse themes because I get absorbed in the sadness. Often, I don't let on about how I feel. Have you had a similar experience?

There's a risk involved in exposing your true feelings because emotions are fluid—they flow and change. They can be like music: rising and falling, growing louder, and then fading away. No two people read the exact same book or hear the exact same song, because we all react to the world with our own point of view. Exposing our emotions can seem like a dangerous risk because we don't know what others will think or how they will react to us, and that can spark anxiety. But the problem with anxiety is that if we try to hold it down, it tends to grow. Anxiety fights back, demanding to be looked in the face and reckoned with.

DREAM UP NOW ⬆

So what can you and I do with anxiety? Let's throw all our worries into the fire.

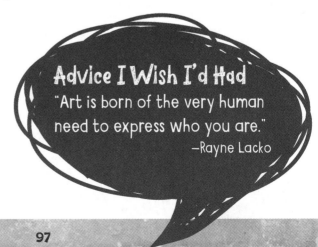

Advice I Wish I'd Had
"Art is born of the very human need to express who you are."
—Rayne Lacko

I Feel . . . Anxious

Grab a pencil, pen, or colored pencils. In the flames below, begin writing or sketching out everything you are worried about.

Holding your anxiety down is like trying to push a beach ball underwater. You'll only create pressure and make it pop right back up. Instead of pushing your worries down, let's burn them all up. Don't lift your hand until all your worries are out of your head and on the page.

If you need help now, or if your anxiety feels too big to manage on your own, I encourage you to talk to someone you trust or reach out to one of the hotlines or apps in the resources section of this journal.

Share your art
@dreamupnowjournal
#dreamupnow.

Want to dig deeper?

There may be a lot going on in your life right now that can cause anxiety. Take a moment to be mindful. Try to silence the noise and focus in on what *you* want.

Write or draw a secret you wish you could tell the world.

What meaningful challenge do you hope to accomplish?

What would you do if you were invisible?

What do you hope to see in your future?

Who would you like to spend more time with?

What habit do you wish you could break?

I FEEL . . . PASSIONATE

courage / pursuing goals / finding joy /
helping others / standing up for your beliefs

Meet Rayne Lacko

Pursuing the things that give you the most energy and enthusiasm is essential to a life of joy and fulfillment. Whether it's taking the scary first steps on the road to your dreams, trying out for a sports team or part in a play, or simply mustering the courage to have a difficult conversation with a friend or an adult in your life, you are often called to "perform." Rayne confides her secret mantra for pursuing her goals passionately and presents a game plan for juggling anxiety with acts of courage. (For more about Rayne, see page 96.)

But what if you haven't discovered where your true strengths and talents lie? Rayne offers straightforward advice for manifesting a passionate life.

Rayne Shares

Before my passion found me, I never even considered teaching teens or writing Young Adult (YA) books. When I was a kid, I had many career dreams, but the two ongoing ones were 1) becoming a rock star, and 2) making my literary mark on the world. As an introvert with an off-pitch singing voice and a bad case of stage fright, the rock star fantasy hasn't exactly panned out.

A few years back, I was on the board of a literary event–planning organization, and one of the members asked me if I'd take over for her as a teen writing mentor. This person was a brilliant writer, but first and foremost my friend. I couldn't say no because of my deep respect for her.

Discovering what the teen writers in the workshop were working on, I found their ideas refreshingly original, honest, and vulnerable. Whatever fears I had about getting up in front of a class were forgotten, because I wanted to walk with each writer through his/her/their journey and to see their stories come to "The End." I was hooked. Working with teens lit me up, inspired me, and reinvigorated my own writing. I switched gears and started writing alongside them, focusing on the YA category.

I found that I receive more joy in helping other people be creative than I do from pursuing my personal goals. Making other people's lives amazing is among the most powerful pleasures known to humankind.

So I found other ways for the writers to shine, creating Teen Creatives Live, an open mic event, with my friends at my local library. The more you give of yourself and try things that are "scary," the more you'll find what matters to you, and the clearer you'll be about the life you wish to create.

Don't know what you're passionate about yet? All through high school, teens have a ton of pressure around what the future holds. I encourage you to give up waiting for the perfect gig or the one thing you think you can stick with forever. Taking a job (any legitimate paying position) gets you unstuck. Going to college (for anything you don't abjectly hate) gets you unstuck. Volunteering (in any capacity for a worthy cause you believe in) gets you unstuck.

Choosing to commit to something gives you a reason to get up in the morning and a place to go where people need you. It's totally okay not to know what you'll be doing a few years from now because the most fulfilling passions are those that find you.

Let me tell you a little secret. Passion is contagious. When you're fully present and giving yourself to whatever task you're doing, people around you notice and want in on your good vibes. Passionate people are drawn to passionate people.

As an introvert, I am terrified (every time!) of standing up in front of the class. But I'm more afraid of missing out on something that brings me real and lasting happiness. So I have a little mantra I tell myself: *anxiety, or it didn't happen.*

I look at anxiety as a badge of honor. It means I got out there and did something that scared me. Believe me, I've accomplished all I can inside my comfort zone. Everything good that I want is outside my comfort zone. I had to decide to stop craving comfort all the time to find my passion.

DREAM UP NOW ⬆

Keeping in mind that you aren't locked in forever, try giving your 100 percent enthusiasm and interest when working at your part-time job, doing your homework, practicing a musical instrument or sport, or even when helping with the laundry—just as an experiment to see what happens.

Act like your life depends on it, like you're making a difference, and like your part counts, because in reality it does—for you. Whether there are external rewards or not, you'll get your own reward. You'll build a passionate life, and you'll find out what is or isn't your thing, because you gave it your all. For more advice on finding your passion, check out the online leadership guide at freespirit.com/dream.

Let's make a game plan to take the scary first steps on the road to your dreams. Any time you feel anxious, remember to give the very best of you.

Advice I Wish I'd Had
"You are the creator of your world. Embrace who you are by doing what brings you joy."
–Rayne Lacko

I Feel . . . Passionate

First, define your goal. (Examples: try out for a sports team or a part in a play, volunteer at an animal shelter, go on a job interview, have a difficult conversation with a friend, family member, or teacher.)

My goal is _____.

Now, find a quiet place and say the following statements out loud to yourself, repeating them until it feels comfortable. Then in the space provided, write a personal note to yourself of any other reminders that will help you feel more confident.

Dedication. I commit to show up on time, with everything I need to take steps to achieve my goal. I commit to being fully present and 100 percent enthusiastic.

Feel the fear and do it anyway. I accept that anxiety is part of my process. I'm glad I am bigger than my fears. Things will happen that are outside my control and that is a natural part of life. How I react is my choice.

Practice, practice, practice. I don't have to be perfect. Every time I take steps toward achieving my goal, it is practice for the next time I do it. Everything I experience is part of my learning process.

Confidence with self-care. I want to feel my best. Paying attention to my posture, hygiene, and grooming shows that I respect and care for myself and gives me more confidence.

Walk in with a smile. My facial expression sets the tone. If I look mad or "meh," others will mirror me. If I smile, others are more likely to smile back, which will help me feel more welcome.

Give thanks. I show my gratitude in all things. I am the director of my day. I choose to honor this opportunity I've been given. I'm thankful when others give me a chance. In gratitude and in love, I walk this path.

I have something of value to offer. I am here to be fully and completely me, just as I am, at this point in my life. Part of learning who I am requires me to go out into the world to try new things.

Personal Note to Self:

Share your art @dreamupnowjournal #dreamupnow.

I FEEL . . . ANGRY

jumping to conclusions / lashing out / explosive behavior / lack of justice

Meet Gem Seddon

"I always knew I was gay," Gem says, but she felt angry because she had zero support as a teen for discovering what "being gay was about." She had no resources available to her through her local community, and no one she dared to talk to about it. Learning about homosexuality was banned in Derby, England, where Gem grew up. During her teen years, the UK enacted the Section 28 clause, making it illegal to "promote the teaching in any school of the acceptability of homosexuality as a pretended family relationship." Gem felt alone. She kept her secret for years, finally coming out to her mom when she was 17. "I didn't tell my dad because I was terrified," she says. She was so accustomed to hiding her true self because she was told by everyone in her community that being gay wasn't "normal." Her father found out when she was 19. "He wanted me to feel open enough to trust him," she says. Today, Gem and her wife live in a welcoming community and receive "open support from people of all ages who support each other through all kinds of life journeys."

Gem is a teen librarian who creates unique, creative, and interactive events and programs for young people. For 15 years, she performed in bands as a professional drummer and taught music. She also plays guitar and violin. For the past eight years, she's reported on movies and TV as a freelance entertainment writer. Gem now lives with her wife and their dog on an island in Washington, where she indulges her love of baking delicious treats. Gem received her master's in library science from Loughborough University and her B.A. in film and creative writing from the University of Derby. Learn more about her on Twitter @gem_seddon.

Gem Shares

I believe anger and tolerance go hand in hand. All through school, I felt a lack of tolerance toward me that ignited an anger even I didn't fully understand. I was bullied from grades 7 to 10. I had to move homerooms twice. I had "friends" who claimed to be open-minded and accepting of me, but those very people never stuck up for me when I was being bullied or when others were being intolerant toward me.

One unfortunate incident occurred when my homeroom signed me up for running at the all-school sports day. I ended up at a track event with the entire school, with all the parents and teachers watching, doing the 1,500-meter run. I was going so slowly that I was lapped by two other girls and it looked like I came in third when I was actually far behind. As I "crossed the finish line," the coach was impressed and wouldn't listen to me explain that I hadn't come in third. From the bleachers, the entire school started a slow, whispered chant: *cheater, cheater, cheater*. It got louder and louder. I remember this so vividly. I was hurt, upset, and totally mortified.

To deal with the pain of feeling angry, I found peace spending time alone. I started playing violin when I was 8, then guitar at age 10, and drums at 11. I poured my feelings into music and into writing in my journal. In my teens, I played drums in rock bands and in the school bands. Playing music made me feel like there was a place for me in the world. Bullying and bad words couldn't reach me. I started to rely on myself and became more self-determined. If I wanted to improve my ability to do a four-stroke roll on the drums really quickly, there was no one who could stand in my way. Music gave me a sense of free will. To this day, playing music gives me a feeling unlike any other, a euphoria. Music gives me peace, and the unwavering knowledge that I'm where I'm meant to be.

Channeling the anger I feel toward others into my creative endeavors has made me a better writer and musician—and ultimately has brought an emotional authenticity to everything I create. Even if it's not an angry piece of writing or music, the fact that I've persevered through tough experiences has made me more creative, more expressive, more determined to be exactly who I am. Anger is as real as joy, and those ups and downs are part of being a creative person.

DREAM UP NOW ⬆

I used to get really pissed off when people couldn't accept me for who I am. I guess I still do sometimes. I know now that anger isn't bad and isn't good; *it just is*. You're going to feel anger. That's okay. But you can make peace with it when you use your creativity. Let's look at what's making you angry, create a boundary word to help you cool off, and then brainstorm ways to channel your feelings into creativity.

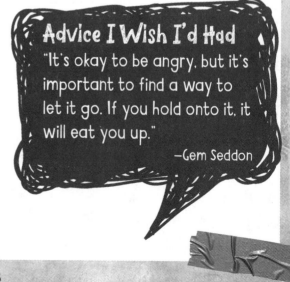

Advice I Wish I'd Had
"It's okay to be angry, but it's important to find a way to let it go. If you hold onto it, it will eat you up."

—Gem Seddon

I Feel . . . Angry

As you think about how anger affects you, and how to create more peacefulness within yourself and your life, try these three tips:

Tip 1: Write down everything you can think of that angers or frustrates you.

Tip 2: Choose a boundary word. Before we can choose peace or kindness (or anything that doesn't involve lashing out at the person we're angry with), it's helpful to set a safe boundary. Using pens, colored pencils, or collage, draw a word that helps you cool off from your anger. Choose a boundary word that represents what you want, such as *kindness*, *protection*, *patience*—or maybe this is the right time to simply create a giant NO. Being able to say no firmly and directly is an essential skill for cultivating self-respect and honest communication.

Tip 3: Create a plan for resolving your anger. Take a good look at your list from Tip 1. How many of those things could you resolve right now if you took the time? For each item you listed, write down one positive action you can take. It can be as simple as writing a letter, having a conversation, going for a walk or run, listening to or playing music, writing in a journal, drawing, meditating, or playing a game. Keep it simple so you can get started easily.

If you need more help or would like someone to talk to about your anger, reach out to a hotline or app listed in the resource section at the end of this journal.

Share your art
@dreamupnowjournal
#dreamupnow.

I FEEL . . . TOLERANT

kindness toward self / kindness toward others /
acceptance / patience / compassion

Meet Gem Seddon

Gem was isolated as a teen because her community banned all resources and information about homosexuality. Today, she supports the dramatic shift of positivity and acceptance toward LGBTQ+ people (and others who are often oppressed) in the media, in TV and movies, online, and in literature. (For more about Gem, see page 105.) She is an advocate in her community and has created an encouraging, safe space for all young people in the library where she works. Gem believes that, regardless of our circumstances, our parents' beliefs, or what our community is telling us, we are free to share our authentic selves and accept others for who they are. "We are moving away from old ideas about how people should be," she says, "but there is still work we need to do."

Gem Shares

Tolerance is being considerate of people, even when you don't know what's happening to them in their personal life. It's easy to be nice and supportive and friendly toward people who are pleasant to you. What I've learned is that when someone is being intolerant, more often than not it's because they are hurting, or because they only know part of a situation and it seems bad, or because they are basing their decisions in fear. When someone is acting that way, my gut reaction is to match that energy—which means I become intolerant in return. In order to practice tolerance, I must choose to focus on being who I am: a kind person.

Practicing tolerance means being patient and taking time to figure out why someone is acting the way they are. One time when someone was mean to me, rather than getting mean back, I talked to her and found out her dog had just died. She was deeply hurt and just needed a moment of kindness. Of course, some people are not hurting from a specific event, but instead make a habit of showing meanness. It's so easy to slip and match that person's negativity, but I have decided to live with peace and tolerance.

Other people may choose to be unkind until the day they die, but I won't. And I won't bend or change to make people treat me better. Accepting someone does not mean approving of their behavior. Their behavior is their choice; my behavior is mine. I have set a boundary for how I choose to be, and I uphold it so I can live in peace.

If someone is being mean to you, try to have compassion and understanding. Set a boundary for yourself and how you choose to act, and try, difficult as it may be, not to get pulled into the other person's negativity by lashing out. Practicing tolerance means coping with situations and people that are distasteful or that go against your grain in a way that isn't disrespectful or rude. Tolerance allows you to keep moving forward, regardless of whatever difficult thing is happening.

If you are being intolerant toward someone in your school or community, ask yourself: *What if that were my sibling or friend and someone was treating them that way? How would I feel?* The same is true if there is one particular person in class who everyone picks on. It's easy to be tempted to follow along with the group and do what everyone else is doing. If it's making one person feel isolated or alone, imagine if it happened to you or someone you care about.

DREAM UP NOW ⬆

We live in a diverse world. There will always be people who are different from you. How you choose to respond to people's cultures, lifestyles, and worldviews is a personal decision. The activity on the next page helps you explore how you can live a more tolerant life.

Advice I Wish I'd Had

"Do your thing. Go find your place and you do you. Get out of self-pity, and get on with something that feels good to you: writing, music—anything that moves you forward. Don't stay there in the moment of intolerance."

—Gem Seddon

I Feel . . . Tolerant

The next time you're around someone who usually drives you nuts, I suggest you try these two simple things:

1. **Consider that they are who they are, whether or not you like who they are. (That's acceptance!)**

   Regardless of whether I like _____,
   I accept him/her/them.

2. **Despite this challenging relationship, one positive thing I can create is:**

The diagram on page 113 can help you brainstorm ways to respond to intolerance. In the Me circle, write words or draw images that represent you and what you stand for. In the Different Opinion circle, write or draw the ideas and opinions people in your community hold that oppose what you stand for. Then, in the middle, take some time to figure out your Response. How can you respond to these opposing views in a way that helps you live a more peaceful life and respect yourself and others?

HERE ARE SOME IDEAS FOR YOUR RESPONSE CIRCLE:

DO: sports/work out, music, writing, video games, hobbies, hang with supportive friends.

ACT: volunteer, bake cookies for someone, help someone (a friend, grandparent, neighbor), voice your opinion to your local, state, or federal government.

SWITCH: find something to do that is the opposite of your feeling. If you're angry, watch an uplifting movie, read a funny book, or listen to a comedy podcast.

CARE: imagine someone you love is suffering or angry. How would you comfort them? Give that same caring to yourself.

Share your art
@dreamupnowjournal
#dreamupnow.

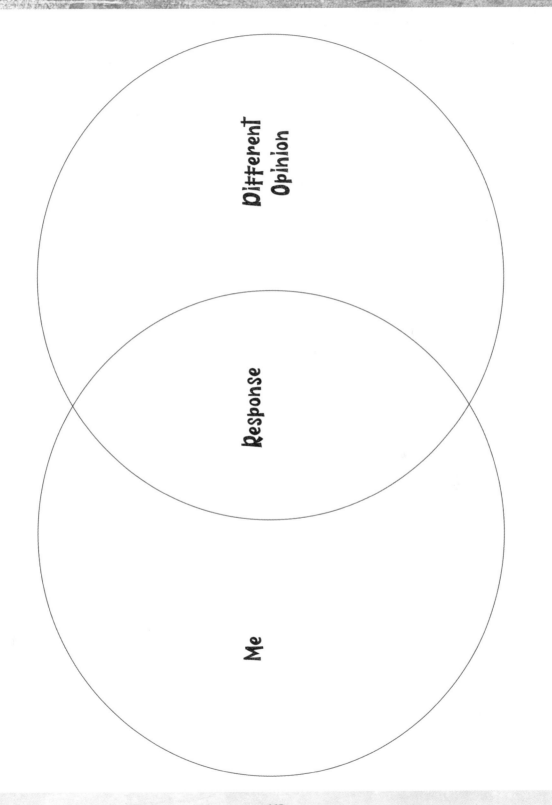

CALM IN A STORM

Cultivating peace, forgiveness, or understanding can sometimes feel easy, and other times requires a lot of work—especially if your world is currently in a state of chaos. Write your name (whatever you prefer to be called) in large, bold letters. Decorate your name using different colors, designs, shadows, or anything you like. Express yourself. Then draw a solid, unbroken circle around your name. This represents you in a safe, protected space. There is nothing outside the circle that can tear you down. You are enough, you are okay exactly how you are, and you are safe. How does it feel to be in this space?

Share your art
@dreamupnowjournal
#dreamupnow.

I FEEL . . . NERVOUS

panic / struggling with self-image / fearing perceived risks /
isolation / avoiding triggers

Meet Sara Bourland

When Sara was a teen, she felt everything so intensely. To her, every new experience seemed bigger than life. Since there was no owner's manual, no guidebook on how to live as a teen, she struggled to figure out what "normal" was supposed to look like. "I had no idea how to temper what I felt and how not to go 100 percent down the rabbit hole of my negative thoughts and feelings." As a result, perfectionism and nerves haunted her. "The concept of being human, that we are hardwired to make mistakes, was not in my understanding yet," Sara says. Her teen years were a painful time.

Sara is a designer, artist, and educator. She has many years of experience as a professional interior designer and has spent the last 14 years teaching English and creative writing to teens in the Pacific Northwest. Sara earned the 2018 Outstanding Educator Award from Delta Kappa Gamma and was named 2010 Teacher of the Year by Veterans of Foreign Wars (VFW) Post 4664. Sara shares her love of designing intentional spaces in a relatable and compassionate way. Her clients experience the power of what an intentional space can do: lower stress, increase confidence, and transform your outlook on life! And as a hands-on artist teaching writing, painting, and metalwork, Sara inspires others to use their creativity as a transformative practice.

Sara Shares

Nervous—it's one feeling I often felt as a teen and continue to struggle with today. Who doesn't? In high school, I rode an exhausting emotional roller coaster. When I was with my friends and the times were good, I felt myself peak with joy and happiness. Then something would happen, and I would immediately crash to the bottom, at breakneck speed. Disappointment and despair were waiting for me.

As a teen, I usually felt nervous or anxious when faced with new situations. Uncharted territory caused my stomach to churn, and then I would go into judgment mode. I'd start to criticize myself, and my head and heart would start to ache. This cycle was relentless. What would begin as nervousness spiraled into self-doubt. I think I had an unrealistic vision of how I should act, behave, perform.

When you think about your emotions and why you feel the way you do, I'd like you to be gentler with yourself than I was. This nervousness you are going through is something that we have all been through. You are not alone.

DREAM UP NOW ⬆

Sit quietly and ask yourself what you want. Think of a trait or quality that would support or improve your current situation. Maybe you need more understanding, compassion, trust, wisdom, or confidence. For me, it was more confidence and self-trust. Whatever idea pops into your mind, trust it. Go with it.

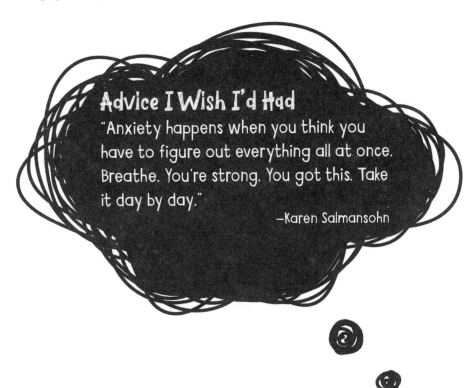

Advice I Wish I'd Had
"Anxiety happens when you think you have to figure out everything all at once. Breathe. You're strong. You got this. Take it day by day."

—Karen Salmansohn

I Feel . . . Nervous

When I felt nervous as a teen, I had an intense need to get my feelings out! Writing helped me deal with everything that was going on inside me. I invite you to try it too. Grab a pencil or pen. Find a private, comfy spot to be alone with your thoughts.

Here are a few writing prompts to get you started. Respond to the prompts you connect with and let go of the ones you don't. But be sure to complete numbers 1, 3, and 6. Express your pain, feel it. Then, in the next step, build a path through it.

Start writing.

1. Why do I feel nervous or anxious?

2. I imagine my emotions are covering me like a blanket. I gently lift a corner and peek out from under it. What is there? What's behind my nervous energy?

3. Am I being too hard on myself? Explain.

4. Who is someone I admire? Why?

5. If they were faced with this situation and nervousness, how would they respond?

6. What qualities do I wish I had that would give me relief from my nervousness?

I FEEL . . . SELF-ASSURED

having faith in yourself / not being swayed by others /
self-pride / able to handle change

Meet Sara Bourland

One thing that always made Sara feel better when she was a teen was rearranging her bedroom. (For more about Sara, see page 116.) She had a creative mind and an eye for color and space, and instead of simply arranging her room to look good, she chose to consider which personal qualities she wished she had and add elements of them to her room. It helped her feel like she had control over her environment. The kinds of qualities she wanted included confidence and the power of feeling self-assured.

She believes making a change to your personal space is the first step in taking control of your situation. Sara says, "Once you know what you want, take steps to make it real for you."

Sara Shares

What helped me gain a sense of self-assurance as a teen—and still does as an adult—is gaining control of my environment. As a teen, that meant rearranging and redecorating my bedroom. My method is easy to learn: I focus on what I can do to transform challenging or uncomfortable feelings into more desirable ones. Turning my attention to changing my environment alleviates negative, nagging feelings and distracts my mind by focusing it on something concrete and constructive. I'm certain it will do the same for you. Plus, changing your environment moves the energy of the space and can alter how you view your situation. More importantly, improving your space is a form of self-care. If you are feeling uneasy, self-care is exactly what you need!

Taking action, even a small action, reinforces the belief that you are in charge of your circumstances. You can take control and make changes. It starts with the physical—taking control of your space—and then you can move on to tackle your internal landscape. To begin, it's okay to just think about a practical need. Maybe what you need is simply to organize your backpack. Cleaning and decluttering are great first steps.

DREAM UP NOW

What quality would you like to gain? Perhaps it is a sense of commitment, persistence, initiative, concentration, patience, or confidence. As you begin to organize or rearrange your space, imagine that you are infusing the quality you desire into it. Keep your desired quality in mind and let this time be just for you. Know that it will be healing.

Advice I Wish I'd Had

"When the world is feeling unkind, you need a space that nurtures you. Give yourself the gift of a space that is your own retreat. You deserve a space that allows you to be yourself and recharge."

—Sara Bourland

I Feel . . . Self-Assured

The best place to begin a transformation is within your own environment. If you have your own room, this is easy. If you share a room, change just your personal space. There are two options:

- Option 1: Clean Up and Organize
- Option 2: Enhance Your Space

Not sure which one to do? Ask yourself: Is my space disorganized? Do I have difficulty finding what I'm looking for? If the answer is yes to either of these questions, start with Option 1. Otherwise, begin with Option 2.

Option 1: Clean Up and Organize

1. Start small. Begin with a closet or desk drawer.
2. Gather three boxes or bags. One for trash, one for recycling, and one for donations.
3. Sort every piece you have into three piles: keep, donate, or throw away/recycle.
4. Put items in your keep pile back in place in an organized, logical way. It must make sense to you so that you can find what you want later. This process may take a while, so tackle only what you can finish in one session. For example, you may only be able to do your sock drawer and save the other dresser drawers for another day.
5. Remove the items in the donate and throw away/recycle piles from your space.
6. Step back and savor the improvements!

The more you do, the better you will feel. It will take time, but your desired changes will come about as you intentionally improve your personal space.

Option 2: Enhance Your Space

1. Again, start small. Choose one section to start.
2. Choose one category from the Ideas for Change list on pages 123–124 and try adding items from this category to your space.
3. Work toward adding more categories from the Ideas for Change list to your personal space. It takes some effort, so just do one at a time.

IDEAS FOR CHANGE	QUICK & EASY DIRECTIONS	MY PLAN
Words Whatever you do, you just need to see those positive messages every day.	Search for quotes that speak to what you are building in yourself. Type or draw your favorite quotes or great sayings. Choose words or messages that are positive and feed you. If you've received a loving message from someone close to you, hang it in your space. Sometimes, it's easier to accept reassuring words if they come from someone else. Frame the message or pin it to a bulletin board.	
Images Surround yourself with happy images. Smile. Look at these positive images daily.	What makes you smile or fills you with joy? Pictures of animals or nature? Your favorite sport? Photos with your friends? Draw or print some favorite images and frame them or pin them to a bulletin board.	
Symbols Symbols represent various qualities. Some are religious, some cultural.	Search for symbols that give you strength, resilience, persistence, or any other quality you wish to build in yourself. Spirals, crosses, and infinity symbols are popular. Draw your symbols or print them. Frame them or pin them to a bulletin board.	

IDEAS FOR CHANGE	QUICK & EASY DIRECTIONS	MY PLAN
Sounds Surround yourself with music to match your many different moods.	What music fills you with strength, joy, or happiness? Are there songs that help you feel peaceful or calm? Be sure you have uplifting playlists for those times when you need a boost.	
Touch Your space should provide you with physical comfort when you are in need.	What about the texture of your space? Sounds weird, I know. Maybe you want a fuzzy blanket to wrap yourself in when you need a hug or to have a good cry. You can also bring the outdoors in. Add a plant, a beautiful rock, or a feather.	
Visual Organizing and putting away items has a way of clearing the mind.	How does your space appear from outside? Is it neat and tidy? Does it make you feel good about yourself? If not, straighten up so you know where you stuff is located. This will help you feel in control.	
Scent Banish stale odors; welcome freshness.	Does your space smell nice? Open the window, vacuum, and air it out.	

Share your art
@dreamupnowjournal
#dreamupnow.

I FEEL . . . DISORGANIZED

feeling confused & overwhelmed / chaotic schedule /
struggling with self-image / forgetfulness

Meet Lesley Holmes

It was easy for Lesley to feel disorganized as a teen because she was trying to balance a lot. She often felt like her life was spinning out of control. There were always too many things to do and never enough hours in the day. Growing up working in her family's restaurant, there were plenty of responsibilities but usually little money, so Lesley would take on babysitting jobs (more work) to buy the things she needed for school. Finding time to organize herself and her thoughts was difficult. She felt a lot of pressure to be "the responsible one" in situations at school, at work, with her boyfriend, and in friendships. She never took the time to be a kid, she never took the time to play, and she was always expected by adults to take the lead.

Lesley realizes the integral need for creative outlets for young people and adults. She has spent the last decade helping seniors and children improve their quality of life. She established the Michael Jackson Music Education Lab at her daughters' elementary school in Hollywood, California, giving every student the opportunity to learn to play the piano. Her leadership roles in various nonprofit organizations help build strong communities and improve the lives of seniors and kids through creative programs.

Lesley Shares

I have always felt like an adult. Even as a teen, I felt like I had the responsibility of the world on my shoulders. At the age of 15, I felt the pressures of school, work, finances, and social and family relationships. Even though I kept a pretty good schedule and created a general to-do list, my head was constantly spinning. I felt like one day spun into the next and that my to-do list kept growing and growing. I never seemed to be able to check anything off.

I felt disorganized much of the time. I kept thinking, "If I just work harder, or study longer, everything will be fine." What I eventually realized was that I was prioritizing everything but me. I put others before me because I thought they were more important and that I didn't matter. I often was hard on myself and put myself down. What I realize now is how important kindness is, and this includes being kind to yourself.

DREAM UP NOW ⬆

Most people feel disorganized and shuffled at times. I know I do. Feeling disorganized can be tough because there's not always a clear starting point for getting everything straightened out. It's easy to get distracted when you're disorganized. Creating a Shuffle Slam will get you through it and help you discover how to begin getting organized.

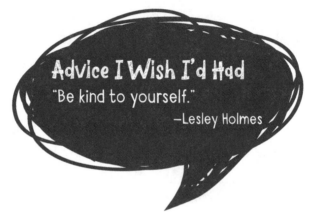

Advice I Wish I'd Had
"Be kind to yourself."
—Lesley Holmes

I Feel . . . Disorganized

I'd like you to write a Shuffle Slam about something that makes you feel disorganized. I'll help you get started. Your Shuffle Slam can be poetry, rap lyrics, or spoken word. This easy process allows you to give your messy thoughts some order, and a rhythm. Honestly, it's pretty fun too. Your Shuffle Slam is just for you. You don't have to read it to anyone except yourself.

Think about what makes you feel disorganized. What pressures and responsibilities do you have that feel chaotic or just a hot mess? What can you not stand? Is it piles of papers? Is it homework, family expectations, or friendships? Does your mind sometimes go from one thing to another? Think about it. What has to change—now? Let's Shuffle Slam it!

Step 1: Take every chaotic thought, situation, or memory and write them all down. Use this space to think of words, phrases, and sentences.

Step 2: Read it all out loud. Use the voice memo on your phone to record your chaos. Say it to a rhythm, by tapping your foot or using one of your hands to pat your chest, your thigh, or the table.

Step 3: Take your raw, random words and sentences and delete anything that doesn't feel right. Add any parts you forgot to say. Make it clear which things are really bugging you. Put everything in an order that makes sense to you. It doesn't have to rhyme. Just get the chaos out of your head and onto the page.

Step 4: It's time to spice up your writing. Try a simile, "My chaos is like . . ." or a metaphor, which is an image that represents what's going on in your head.

Step 5: Write your final Shuffle Slam in the space below, and then read it out loud. Find your rhythm and let it all out!

Share your art
@dreamupnowjournal
#dreamupnow.

I FEEL . . . ORGANIZED

managing homework / letting go of chaos /
calm / better time management

Meet Lesley Holmes

Feeling organized can be very satisfying. As a teen, Lesley learned to see how getting organized helped improve her outlook on life. (For more about Lesley, see page 125.) She knows
teens are exposed to a lot of expectations and pressures, usually several at one time. It
can seem as if there is a constant stream of negative information. Receiving so many negative messages is exhausting. It often can feel like you're too tired to stay on top of what's
important to you. Lesley likes to look for the positive in a negative situation. Finding the
positive requires acknowledging that bad things happen while remaining open to goodness.
She believes there is always a silver lining.

Lesley Shares

As a teen, I had a great relationship with my grandparents. My great-grandmother
and I had a ritual during my teen years. We would put all our spare change into an
empty cottage cheese container. When it was full, we'd organize it into bankable rolls
of coins, usually netting about $50 that would otherwise be overlooked or never spent.
A series of small habits can add up a worthwhile payoff, like choosing healthier foods
or practicing an instrument or sport. What small habit can you start that will benefit
you in the long run?

A simple method I use for keeping myself organized is Four Quadrants. To do this,
simply draw four squares on a page and mark them: What I Need Now, What I Need
Tomorrow, What I Need This Week, and What I'm Working Toward in the Future.

When I was saving for my first car, Four Quadrants would have helped me realize
that I wasted too much money on things like fancy coffee and junk food. If I'd been
honest about how much money I actually needed to spend each day and chose not to
spend on things I could live without, I would have saved faster. Four Quadrants works
great for homework too. It's easy to get so caught up with worry about a big homework assignment that's due next week, that you forget to complete a small assignment
due in the morning. Four Quadrants helps you make your goals clear.

I'm still learning new organization skills. For example, I recently learned to play guitar. It used to feel like it took forever to learn a new song. When I struggle too much, I often want to give up. So I decided to learn only one measure of a song at a time. Because one measure is a manageable small goal, I learn it much faster. By the time I get to the last measures of a song, I can play the whole song confidently and have fun with it. To swim across the pool, you take one stroke at a time.

DREAM UP NOW ⬆

If you're ready to get control over your chaos, I'll share some helpful, effective tools for getting organized that are teen-tested and really work. Let's sort out everything you need to do on Get-It-Together Trees, then choose the best tools for each task. Get started now.

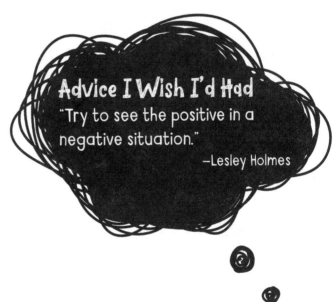

Advice I Wish I'd Had
"Try to see the positive in a negative situation."
—Lesley Holmes

I Feel . . . Organized

Drawing a Get-It-Together Tree is a fun and artistic way to get organized. It's so easy and quick that you can draw one tree for every chaotic or messy issue you talked about in your Shuffle Slam.

Begin with the sample Get-It-Together Tree on page 134. On the trunk, write one of the pressures or responsibilities you talked about in your Shuffle Slam. On each leaf, choose actions from the Get Organized List below that will help resolve the problem, get you back on track, or create a new way of handling it.

Make as many trees as you need to figure out how to organize each of the items that have you feeling disorganized. These simple tree visuals will help you gain control of your responsibilities and can be re-created or updated any time!

GET ORGANIZED LIST

CALENDAR IT. Got an upcoming deadline or appointment? Whether you add a note in your phone's calendar or use a physical planner, calendar, or whiteboard in your room, put all your important responsibilities where you'll see them.

USE YOUR PLANNER. Your planner is only taking up room in your backpack if it isn't getting put to good use. Take it out at the end of every class and write down your homework assignments. Note any due dates. Each night, take out your planner and read what you wrote.

CLEAN. Empty out every pocket and every compartment of your backpack. Get out all the trash and unneeded items. You'll find some missing items, guaranteed. Do the same with your closet, under your bed, and that one drawer where you put random stuff.

PUT AWAY TECH. It can be hard to effectively focus on the task at hand if you're also checking social media, texting friends, or watching videos online. Commit to tuning out these distractions (and putting away any screens you don't actively need) while completing a goal. Just focus on the one thing you're doing. You'll be amazed at how much work you can get done when you're not distracted.

COLOR-CODE. Choose a specific color folder or binder for each class or task and stick everything related to that class or task in its folder. This will help you keep track of the materials you need.

BREAK IT DOWN. If you have an elephant-sized task, break it down to bite-sized pieces. Begin at the beginning. Be patient and keep going until you're done.

PLAN. Pick a time on Sunday to write down in your planner or calendar everything you need to do in the coming week. Ask a friend or adult for help if you need it.

SPEEDWORK. Engineers and programmers know that humans can only maintain solid focus for 25 minutes at a time. Set an alarm for 25 minutes, then laser-focus on whatever you want to get done. When the alarm goes off, take a 5-minute break to check your messages or get a snack, then do another 25 minutes of focused work if needed.

USE FOUR QUADRANTS. Draw four squares on a page and mark them: What I Need Now, What I Need Tomorrow, What I Need This Week, and What I'm Working Toward in the Future. Figure out what you need to do, save, or prioritize based on your immediate and long-term goals.

REWARD YOURSELF. If you have a great week and complete all the goals or tasks in your calendar, reward yourself! Your reward could be screen time, hanging with friends, working out, savoring a favorite snack or treat, or whatever feels good to you.

Share your art
@dreamupnowjournal
#dreamupnow.

I FEEL . . . DOUBT

feeling insecure / holding back / lack of confidence / negative self-talk

Meet Angie Godfrey

Just before Angie entered high school, her parents moved the family from their remote dairy farm to a nearby town where she didn't know anyone. At the age of 13, Angie was surrounded by unfamiliar classmates. "I didn't know where I fit in," she says. "I felt I should just blend into the background because I was boring and had nothing to contribute." Angie had been learning to play piano for four years and found that making music gave her comfort. Music was her safe place, where she had control over herself and over what she created. "I enrolled in as many music classes as I could, playing alto sax in school concert bands and piano in jazz band," she explains. "I knew music was natural for me. I knew I could count on it." Angie shows you how allowing yourself to find and nurture your strengths can help you conquer your doubt—and find your place to shine.

Angie has been playing piano since she was 10 years old and alto saxophone since high school, and she's been a certified music teacher for 18 years. She plays a stunning array of instruments and teaches students ages 4–18 to sing and play instruments at a private Montessori school and as the artistic director of a youth choir. Angie graduated from the University of Victoria in Canada with a degree in music education.

Angie Shares

When I started high school in a new town, it took me a while to find where I fit in. The social game was intense. At home, my parents were busy trying to navigate our new dairy farm. Every morning they milked the cows in the barn, so I had to get my younger siblings up, make them breakfast, and get them to school. When I got home after class, it was the same. My parents were tending to the cows, so my sister and I had to start dinner for the family while balancing homework, piano lessons, and sports activities. We learned from an early age that we all had to pitch in with chores and farm work. Sometimes I doubted that I could handle it all. My parents would notice me struggling on hard days and my mom would say, "Why don't you go downstairs and practice piano?"

When playing, I had control over the music, and control over my body. I'd start out bubbling over with stress or self-doubt, but then the music would take over. An hour would fly by, and then another. And by the time I came away, I'd feel total relief and peace. Getting lost in my music was the only way I was able to let out my feelings. When I began playing in the school bands, I was new to high school and doubtful about my musical skills in a larger group. It was different from playing piano by myself, and I worried I'd make mistakes and be embarrassed. I wondered, *What could I do to help myself?*

The truth is you can do far more to help yourself than you might think. There will always be struggles, but if you stop at the first bump, you'll never progress. With music, hitting that bump might mean it doesn't sound good or that you're not connecting with the people in the room or with your teacher. Each day, I was figuring out how to overcome self-doubt and form connections with other kids at my new school. I worried about being judged, but I didn't want that to stop me from showing others my talents. I've performed in countless ensembles, and I've come to discover that everyone else in the room has something they're dealing with. They're counting on you to get better, so they can get better too. Keep going, keep practicing, get to the place you want to be. By honoring your talents and strengths, you can overcome your own self-doubt.

DREAM UP NOW ⬆

Your doubt can be a signal that you're worried about how well you'll perform or that you may not believe in yourself or your skills. Are you holding yourself back with negative self-talk? One of the best ways to overcome doubt is to create a sense of belonging among like-minded people. I will show you how to set a goal to do more of something you love or to do something you've always wanted to try.

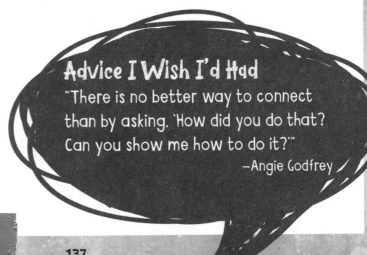

Advice I Wish I'd Had
"There is no better way to connect than by asking, 'How did you do that? Can you show me how to do it?'"

—Angie Godfrey

I Feel . . . Doubt

Think about the thing you're doubting you will do well. Sometimes we focus too much on what could go wrong. Take a moment to instead think about how the situation or event could go exceptionally well. Write or draw in the space below what it would be like to do this thing so well that you feel valued.

Doubts are crushed when you accept where you are, but also set a goal for what you want to achieve. Find inspiration, and then let yourself be inspired! Ask yourself: *What decision can I make to help myself?* In the left-hand column of the chart on the next page, list specific achievable goals to help improve an area in which you feel doubt. (Examples: choose to cooperate with others, show up for practice, show up for tryouts, improve current skills, learn new skills, visualize success, be kind to yourself, read or study as much as possible about your desired topic, allow yourself to make mistakes, find a role model or mentor, take note of what your role model does well and try it your-self, take a leadership role, keep your head up, power pose, practice, practice, practice.)

Now that you know what you want and how you're going to achieve it, I invite you to make a plan. In the right-hand column of the chart, write out how you will help yourself. (Examples: add reminders in my calendar to practice; set a deadline to learn a new technique, skill, or performance piece; set aside a certain amount of time each day or week to learn more about my desired topic; talk to someone I would like to have as a mentor; try out for a team, band, or performance group.)

MY GOAL	MY PLAN

Want to dig deeper? Ask yourself: *How will my goal allow me to form strong and safe connections with others?*

Share your art
@dreamupnowjournal
#dreamupnow.

I FEEL . . . VALUED

belief in self / feeling welcome & wanted /
deepening friendships / improving talents

Meet Angie Godfrey

A sense of being valued comes from positive connections to others. Being valued is very different from being needed. Sometimes you might be needed to complete a difficult or even unpleasant task. But when you respect, admire, or love the person asking you to complete the task, being needed can help you feel valued. Growing up, Angie's journey to gaining a sense of her personal value involved daring to share herself with others—and being patient and open to what others brought her. (For more about Angie, see page 136.) By joining extracurricular activities, she learned to feel valued.

Music was important to Angie, so she made an effort to sign up for various music groups and bands at school, even when she didn't know anyone there. "When I first joined the choir, I sat in the back," she admits. Inspired by the courage of the other choir members, Angie valued the mutual trust and friendship of creating music together and realized she had been missing this feeling of connection. Before long, she moved herself to the front row and began auditioning for solos. Her sense of value grew because of the shared admiration among the group members. Angie can show you how to cultivate a feeling of being valued in a group that is important to you.

Angie Shares

For me, part of feeling valued is feeling like I fit in. I've found that I need to value others to feel valued myself. Having something to strive for and feeling proud of my accomplishments has been important in all stages of my life. Growing up, I lived on a remote farm, and there weren't any kids around. I didn't even go to kindergarten. I was feeling isolated, but through music, I was able to form connections. When I first started high school in a new town, I didn't know anyone, but I knew music was natural for me. I was thankful my school had opportunities for playing music, and I showed my classmates how much I valued them by accompanying our class concerts on the piano. I soon became known at school for my music. My music teacher recognized that these experiences were powerful for me and invited me to direct the band. I accepted the challenge because music gave me that confidence, which is surprising since I was so shy as a kid.

Advice I Wish I'd Had
"Music is not just about you; it's about your entire community. Humans need connection, and music does that in a huge way."
—Angie Godfrey

When you think of the history of music, you think of community. People gathered together to play, sing, and listen to music—to experience it as a group. Every period in history can be defined through its music, which was influenced by what was going on at the time. But I've come to realize that it's not just about the music, it's about who's in the room sharing it with you. The vibrations you create as a group are undeniable; everyone feels it. In high school, music introduced me to students in every grade, people I never would have talked to in the hallways or the cafeteria. All the separate cliques and groups disappeared when we came together to make music. Making music together was this awesome feeling of connection, and it helped us discover each other's talents. People started asking me to play their favorite songs on the piano while they sang the lyrics. I found it difficult to learn songs by ear, but I was inspired when another student would come out of his/her/their comfort zone to ask me. We both had to try. And in the end, our performance gave us both a chance to shine.

If you are longing to deepen your sense of personal value, make new friends, and discover your talents, music is available to you too—whether you perform, create, or just enjoy listening to it. Everyone I performed with in school brought a different contribution—their own unique talent. You don't have to be "good enough" or even play an instrument to show up. Just start with a love of music and go from there. Everyone has to practice, and everyone gets better with practice.

DREAM UP NOW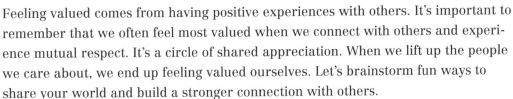

Feeling valued comes from having positive experiences with others. It's important to remember that we often feel most valued when we connect with others and experience mutual respect. It's a circle of shared appreciation. When we lift up the people we care about, we end up feeling valued ourselves. Let's brainstorm fun ways to share your world and build a stronger connection with others.

I Feel . . . Valued

Sharing your interests is a great way to show another person that you care and at the same time increase your sense of personal value. Take a moment to look at the songs you listen to most often on your playlists. The music you most enjoy says a lot about you and reflects your interests and style. Write down the names of three people you'd be willing to share your current favorites with and make a playlist for them.

1. _____

2. _____

3. _____

Is there someone close to you (such as a friend or family member) who is going through a tough time or is struggling with their own doubt? Surprise them by giving them something meaningful—and completely unexpected—using your creativity. You might write a short poem, make a drawing, or invite them to see a local musician, go for coffee, or visit a museum. This will help you both feel valued.

Person I care about: _____

Unexpected thing I can do: _____

Is there a trusted adult who has been there for you? Showing a small token of appreciation isn't always easy, but it has a big impact on those who care. You can do this by just saying thank you. If it feels right to you, consider offering one of the unexpected things listed above. Reflect on a time you felt valued and create a drawing, poem, or thank-you note showing what happened. How did it feel to be valued or to show someone else you value them? See if you can add those feelings into your creation.

Share your art
@dreamupnowjournal
#dreamupnow.

I FEEL . . . CONTROLLING

critical of self & others / domineering / defensiveness / noticing flaws

Meet MaLee Muse

MaLee didn't know she was an artist until she was 25 years old, when a creative friend showed her how to begin and helped her trust that she could do it. It took 10 years for her to let go of doubt and control and to believe in what she was creating. She discovered that everyone is an artist.

When MaLee moved to New York from sunny California, she struggled with her emotions. The extremely cold New York winters can sometimes negatively affect people with a history of depression. Art helped her "be sunny again," she says. She began drawing four connected bubbles in her sketchbook, reflecting on a centered purpose to help her let go of controlling feelings and set clear intentions for her day. Knowing the importance of reaching out and not isolating herself, she added a fifth bubble for connecting to others. Then she added a sixth bubble for physically expressing herself—through reading, painting, cooking, or responsibilities she'd been avoiding. "When I started putting my hopes and responsibilities in bubbles, I could see the equation of happiness," she says.

MaLee is a self-taught artist who has been using her creativity professionally for over 15 years. MaLee studied business in college and started her own marketing company in California before moving to New York and going "off-grid" to live in a tiny house with her husband. A lifelong avid note-taker, MaLee considers herself a "self-help junkie." Her personal studies on how to live her best life helped her establish and develop the Quantum MeMoir technique. You can learn more on youtube.com/MaLeeMuse or on Instagram @QuantumMeMoir.

MaLee Shares

My father was in the military, so I grew up in what I considered to be a very controlling environment. On the military base, if I got in trouble (individually, outside of my family), my dad's boss would get called, and then my dad would get called, all before I got home from school. When your dad gets in trouble, there's a whole lot more trouble for you. There was a rigid expectation that I could never misbehave, could never make a mistake, and that I should be perfect, always. I had to put on airs and use false behavior that wasn't really me. I know now that making mistakes is how we learn. But at the time, pretending to be perfect was how life was for me.

When you are being unforgiving to yourself or demanding perfection of yourself or others, you are being controlling. I was setting exhaustingly high expectations for myself, and I realized I was overbearing, which also means domineering or controlling. What kinds of things are you controlling in your life? Food? Image? Being "good" by someone else's standard and not your own? Demanding certain grades or levels of performance from yourself? Write it here.

For me, controlling looks like _____.

When I became an adult, I started spending time with families and friends outside of the military who were compassionate and who didn't have so many rules and consequences. I began seeing artists, art, and color. That added a lot more dimension to my life and gave me new perspectives. It allowed me to see beyond black and white and appreciate softer edges. I understood that controlling was just one way to be and that mistakes can be beautiful if you are willing to look at life creatively.

If you are experiencing controlling feelings or others have rigid expectations for you, please know that even difficult circumstances can be transformed into a gift. You're gaining strength and resilience that you'll love later in life. I realize now that the challenges I experienced as a teen of moving constantly and living in foreign lands among strangers became some of my greatest gifts. I've learned that I can change behaviors that don't work for me and get a fresh start. As an adult, I've found that this has made it possible for me to take a chance on my dreams and keep improving myself. You can try this with something you are trying to control too.

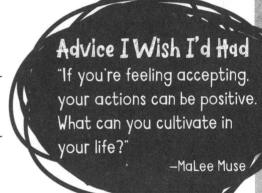

Advice I Wish I'd Had
"If you're feeling accepting, your actions can be positive. What can you cultivate in your life?"
—MaLee Muse

DREAM UP NOW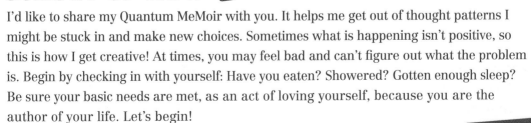

I'd like to share my Quantum MeMoir with you. It helps me get out of thought patterns I might be stuck in and make new choices. Sometimes what is happening isn't positive, so this is how I get creative! At times, you may feel bad and can't figure out what the problem is. Begin by checking in with yourself: Have you eaten? Showered? Gotten enough sleep? Be sure your basic needs are met, as an act of loving yourself, because you are the author of your life. Let's begin!

I FEEL . . . CONTROLLING

To create a Quantum MeMoir, I trace a lid or cup, but I've provided some bubbles for you on the next page. Start with the **Purpose** bubble in the center. Think of the issue you are trying to control and decide what the positive outcome would be. Write it in the bubble. This is your goal.

Intent. Instead of controlling or being controlled, how would this new purpose feel? This desired feeling is now your intent, the thing you want to achieve. Write that feeling or action in the **Intent** bubble. Be sure to write in the present tense. For example, instead of saying, "I will be happy when . . .," claim your purpose and intent for the present moment by writing, "I am peaceful." You want to feel it now. (Feel free to doodle or add extra notes or symbols—whatever feels right to you.)

Observe. Sit quietly without judgment and think about what led you to feel controlling. Think about how you reacted and the kinds of things you did that ended in these controlling feelings or that got you in trouble. Be authentic with yourself and take responsibility for the actions that got you here. Now, create new actions to support your purpose. Be sure to write words and doodles that are positive and compassionate about your circumstances. Start with one observation, any action that will lead to a more positive outcome, and add additional bubbles as you come up with more ideas.

Connect. Authenticity is about being real with yourself and understanding that you are not alone. Other people may have the very same feelings. Think about who can help you reach your purpose. It might be a friend, a parent, a school counselor, or an expert on YouTube. Show gratitude for their help by leaving a reminder of their wisdom in this bubble!

Express. What things can you do to express the purpose you selected? Maybe it's spending time listening to or making music, hanging out with friends, playing a favorite sport, writing poetry, practicing yoga, or eating a healthier diet. If there are more than one or two things, add additional connecting bubbles!

Refine. This is a space to note how you could do better next time. Even after a perfectly happy day, there is always something you can decide to do better tomorrow. If you can't think of anything, compassion is always an excellent feeling to cultivate.

Ground. Show appreciation for what you already have—your strengths, talents, and uniqueness. Take time to be grateful for them. This is how these gifts grow. Embrace your creativity; what makes you, you?

For inspiration, visit @QuantumMeMoir on Instagram to see how colored pencils and doodling outside the lines can help make your Quantum MeMoir an art piece!

Connect

Express

Observe

Purpose

Refine

Intent

Ground

Share your art
@dreamupnowjournal
#dreamupnow.

I FEEL . . . ACCEPTING

forgiveness & compromise / thinking before reacting /
being objective / compassion

Meet MaLee Muse

MaLee has discovered through the daily practice of her Quantum MeMoir that emotions are energy in motion and that by connecting specific "seed" words or bubbles, she can create positive energy in her life. (For more about MaLee, see page 144.) Quantum means any of the very small increments (in this case, bubbles) into which many thoughts can be divided. Using her technique, every piece of energy (each bubble) comes together to create a better life and helps you evolve into a happier person. "I call it a memoir because it's your personal life, your diary," she says.

MaLee shares her Quantum MeMoir method as a way to help you create a colorful, graphic art piece to inspire self-awareness, and she offers the method as a workable plan for living your best life.

MaLee Shares

I've always struggled with proper grammar and spelling, especially in high school. It led me to be self-conscious, afraid I would say or write the "wrong" thing. Since then, I've discovered etymology, which is the history of words—their origins and how their forms and meanings have evolved. Many words and parts of words traveled from one language to another over centuries and have changed over time. The original meaning of many words often turns out to be greatly different than how we use them today. Learning this helped me realize that it's not the word that matters, but the meaning we give it. I gave myself permission to stop relying on another person's words to express what I needed to say. This gave me the freedom to erase, change, or just accept that I make mistakes.

Growing up in the military, I often moved and was around people from all over the world. This experience allowed me to be free from someone else's judgment of how I used a word, because maybe it meant something different where the person came from or to his/her/their community. I decided to let other people understand language the way they do, and I'd understand it for myself. If you observe carefully, you'll see that we speak differently to our friends, to our grandparents, to strangers, or to a coach or teacher. Even the mood we're currently in can change how we communicate.

Language is art; it's an expression of an individual and of a culture or a people. It is reflected in the way we think. To me, this variety is what many call the spice of life!

I learned to accept my perceived "flaw" when I stopped trying to control my need to get my spelling and grammar correct for others. To this day, I rarely use punctuation in my written art, because I'm letting go of things that are expected to be a certain way. I can reinterpret words how I want in my art, because it's an expression of my authenticity.

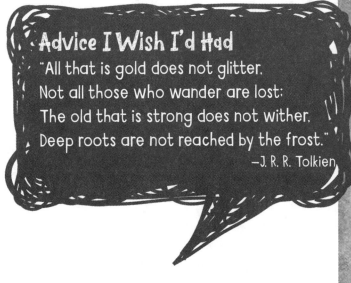

Advice I Wish I'd Had
"All that is gold does not glitter,
Not all those who wander are lost;
The old that is strong does not wither,
Deep roots are not reached by the frost."
—J. R. R. Tolkien

I'm no longer afraid to be judged because I misspelled or used the "wrong" word.

Is there something that makes you feel inadequate compared to other people? Take action and accept yourself for who you are. Make it your intention to look at your "flaw" as your personal signature, your unique means of expression. To do this, you first need to forgive other people for their judgment. Most are asking you to fit into their expectations, because that's what has always been expected of them—which is impossible when you really think about it.

We are born individuals for a reason. Every person has his/her/their own way of doing things, influenced by individual experiences and backgrounds, what their parents taught them, the school they went to, the kind of music they listen to, the era they grew up in, or the country they are from. Let people be who they are. More importantly, love who *you* are.

DREAM UP NOW ⬆

Your mistakes—as well as your strengths—are what make you unique, important, and give you a singular point of view unlike anyone else.

What is the thing you are worried about not doing well? Write it here.

_____

Let's begin a fresh Quantum MeMoir to transform your "flaw" into your personal signature.

I Feel . . . Accepting

Purpose. Remember, only positive thoughts go on your page, so be sure your purpose is positive. In my example, I would put "language" in this bubble instead of "bad grammar" and focus on the artistry of words instead of proper English. Try to see the beauty behind what you are considering a "flaw." You don't have to agree with it yet. That's what the rest of the bubbles are for!

Intent. Write a positive intention or affirmation for what it would feel like to experience your chosen purpose. Your intent is a statement on how you will build self-acceptance.

Observe. Ask yourself: *How did my "flaw" affect me in the past? How did it affect other people?* (Be sure to be compassionate toward yourself and forgive others for their misguided judgment.) This is your chance to rewrite your story. Observing is figuring out what actions work and don't work. This fact-finding will help you choose new behaviors and feelings going forward. Remember, the notes you put here are a positive reminder of what you've experienced.

Connect. Look for positive inspiration and you will find it. Write the name of someone who embraces their unique signature! Reach out and connect with people who inspire you. Create a circle of friends who support your authentic self and do the same for them.

Express. It's time to put action into your new perception. Your strengths and flaws are an expression of you! What different, new, helpful thing are you going to do? Write that in the **Express** bubble, and then get out and do it. Maybe it's something you've never tried before. Be willing to make a choice to try something new!

Refine. Once you realize that every day you can do something better than you did yesterday, you will become more forgiving of yourself and others. Write something that you would like to do better next time.

Ground. Finally, always show appreciation for what you have—your strengths, gifts, and uniqueness.

For inspiration, please visit @QuantumMeMoir on Instagram to see how colored pencils and doodling outside the lines can help make your Quantum MeMoir an art piece!

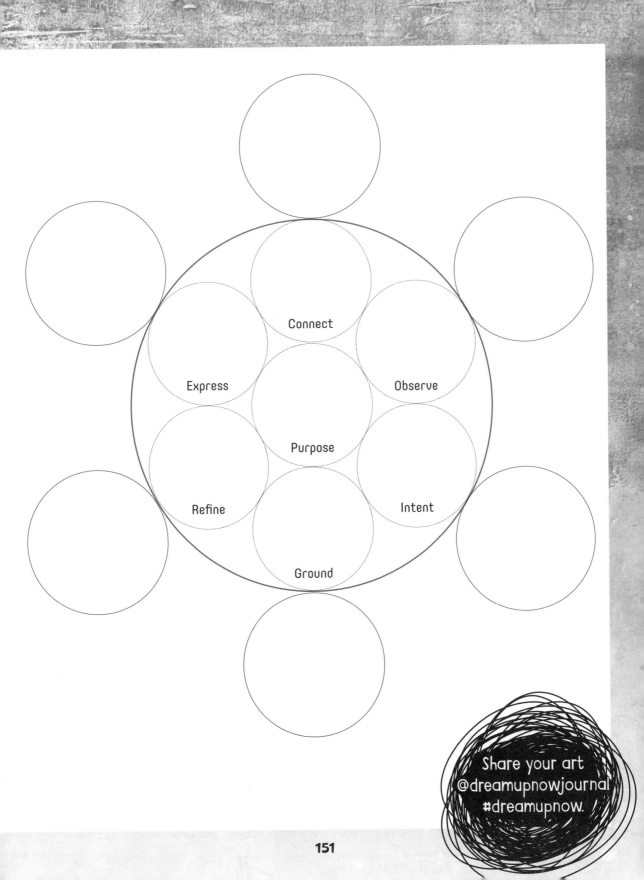

Connect

Express   Observe

Purpose

Refine   Intent

Ground

Share your art
@dreamupnowjournal
#dreamupnow.

ZERO-RISK TEXT

Ever fantasize about telling someone how you really feel? Here's a safe place to get your point across—with zero risk. You decide how the conversation plays out.

Don't know who to text? How about a friend, your mom, someone who died before you had a chance to say what you wanted to say, a celebrity, a political figure, your crush, or maybe a fictional character?

Share your art
@dreamupnowjournal
#dreamupnow.

I FEEL . . . INDECISIVE

needing to please everyone / worried about outcomes /
fear of making mistakes

Meet Melissa Dinwiddie

Melissa lives in a colorful world of painting, calligraphy, playing music, and singing. When she was a teen, she considered herself a "noncreative person," even though she was studying dance and dreamed of one day becoming professional. "I thought other people were the artists, not me," she says. Following her passion for dance, she was accepted to Juilliard and later graduated from UC Berkeley, but she never felt that she'd found her calling. For years after graduating, she felt she was "flailing around, not knowing what to do with myself," even though she was accomplished academically.

One afternoon, she decided to cut little designs into pretty papers and wrap votive candles left over from her wedding to make luminarias. Before long, it was dark outside, but to Melissa, it felt like it had only been five minutes. She says, "Making art was natural and effortless."

Melissa is a painter, calligrapher, paper arts specialist, ukulele player, and jazz singer who offers creative mentorship to working and would-be artists. Melissa has witnessed firsthand that everyone is an artist, which has led her to become an active arts advocate, teacher, and inspirer. Melissa studied social science in gender and society at University of California, Berkeley; spent a year dancing at Juilliard; and earned her master's degree in cultural studies in Birmingham, England. One of her first professional art gigs was creating a ketubah, a Jewish marriage contract. Learn more about Melissa at melissadinwiddie.com or on Instagram @a_creative_life.

Melissa Shares

I grew up in the shadow of Stanford University in California, in a community that worshipped intellect and academic pursuit. It was a high-pressure part of the United States. I had loving parents who were married and working as professionals and who praised me and my brother for being smart and talented. But because I was an

extreme perfectionist, the constant pressure drove me into a fixed mindset. I never gave myself a break. That was really hard. I was always comparing myself to others. I was always expected to "do my best," which was kind of intense. I developed an eating disorder and was not happy. I thought it was normal.

When I discovered myself as an artist, I realized I needed to play. Art needed to be fun again. That's when I established my Creative Sandbox philosophy. Emotions run deep when it comes to our creativity, and we all have creativity scars.

It's time to reclaim the fun and pleasure of working with your hands, drawing and cutting and pasting—whatever brought you joy as a kid, when making arts and crafts was just part of your normal school day.

DREAM UP NOW

Maybe you don't know what kind of art you would like to try, or if you want to try at all. Instead of wasting time worrying or having trouble choosing one thing, remember my number-one guidepost for creativity: *there is no wrong*. This is true for all kinds of pursuits, and it has helped me personally move past being indecisive. *There is no wrong*. Rather than being stuck between choices or unsure of what to do next, I let go of the outcome by thinking process, not product. If you're stuck between two or more choices, I invite you to do the same. Don't worry if what you create will look good or win an award. It's about the fun of trying, of putting yourself into the process and letting go of the outcome.

For your creative spirit to be free to play, it has to be free to do anything—even if that thing is ugly, weird, or stupid. Only once you let go of the fear of "doing it wrong" can your creative spirit let loose.

Advice I Wish I'd Had
"Don't beat yourself up: love yourself up!"

—Melissa Dinwiddie

I Feel . . . Indecisive

Using only a pen or pencil, let's play an improv drawing game. Improv is a style of acting that has no script. One performer makes up a character, says whatever comes to mind, and makes an "offer." The offer could be a gesture or a phrase—anything. The other performer's job is to accept the offer and build on it by responding, "Yes, and . . ."

Together, the performers build a scene from nothing, making up the script as they go along. While getting comfortable with what is happening, they must remain open to what could be. It's a private, personal microcosm, and neither knows how the scene will end.

Every day, you find yourself improvising, because life is filled with uncertainty. We don't always know what's going to happen next and we don't have control over it. So we must be ready to let go of the outcome and be okay with that. You are free to make a decision and allow yourself to be okay with the unknown, open to whatever might happen. Once you see the outcome, then you can make new decisions. Whether it's your art in this journal or improv, however it turns out—good or not so good—you will have learned something. You might learn what not to do next time or what you can develop.

Progress in drawing comes from doing lots of little drawings over time. You'll find out what works, refine your style, and get better and stronger and more creative. It's the same with life. Doing this improv drawing game daily helps you practice letting go of uncertainty and begin making decisions as needed—without worrying about the outcome. Turn to the blank page 156. Now make it un-blank by starting with one mark. It doesn't matter if your mark is a dot or a scribble. Seriously, it does not matter. Just make a mark.

Good. Now it's not a blank page anymore. Next, respond to what's there. In this improv game, the mark is your partner, and the gesture has been made. Accept the reality of what's there and build on it. All you have to do is respond, and then there's a new reality. Accept that reality and expand on it. Don't worry about what your drawing looks like. It's about the fun, the process. Add to this doodle. Remember, *there is no wrong!*

HINT: It's allowed to be imperfect!

Share your art
@dreamupnowjournal
#dreamupnow.

I FEEL . . . DECISIVE

being responsible / choosing to lead / honesty /
building self-esteem / solving problems

Meet Melissa Dinwiddie

Since she is a passionate full-time artist and musician, it's hard to believe that Melissa didn't do any art between the ages of 13 and 28. "I didn't think I was creative," she says. (For more about Melissa, see page 153.)

Melissa believes that if you don't use your own creativity, you'll try to consume other people's creations instead. If you've ever obsessed over designer shoes or jeans, you've been there. When you aren't making your own art (in whatever form lights you up!), you run into the struggle of trying to buy it. "It makes you miserable and it's never enough," she points out. Melissa invites you to make your own creations to feel fulfilled in yourself.

Melissa Shares

When I was a teen, I decided to go to Juilliard. My dance teacher pulled me aside and said, "You should be in New York." This helped me believe in myself. I was 19 years old and a student at UC Berkeley. I'd already invested in and chosen my path, and I didn't know if I'd actually get into Juilliard. I didn't know if dancing would become my career. The audition was a week after classes at UC Berkeley started, so I was either going to miss a week of school or drop out in favor of Juilliard.

I'd never been to New York, and the opportunity to dance wouldn't wait until after graduation. I didn't want to turn 40 one day and wonder what might have been. So I told my parents I wanted to audition. They were shocked because academics were important to them, but they supported me. I choreographed a dance, showed up for the audition on the other side of the country, and got in.

I ended up hating that year at Juilliard. But I'm really glad that 19-year-old me made the decision to try. I thought about the regret I would have felt had I decided not to go for it. The outcome didn't matter!

After that year, I returned to Berkeley and graduated from the program I'd started. I then went to Birmingham, England, to earn my master's degree. That was a big decision too.

DREAM UP NOW

For several years, I was a full-time artist. Now I call myself a creative instigator, which is a different path from what I studied. I allowed myself to dare to pursue my passions at every age, and I invite you to follow your heart as well.

I'm thankful for all the experiences I've had. They gave me the confidence to know that when other wonderful opportunities arise, I'll be okay, no matter the outcome. And so will you.

Advice I Wish I'd Had
Melissa's Golden Formula:
self-awareness + self-compassion =
the key to everything good.

I Feel . . . Decisive

If you're feeling indecisive, ask yourself these questions from Jonathan Fields's book *Uncertainty*:

What's the best thing that could happen?

What's the worst thing that could happen?

What would happen if you do nothing?

I'd like to help you be more decisive. I encourage you to let go of perfectionism and get into the mindspace of being a little kid again. Remember, my number-one guidepost: *There is no wrong*.

Set a timer for two minutes. Now keep your hand moving while you answer two questions. Do not lift your pen from the paper until the timer goes off.

What passion would you pursue if you knew, without a doubt, that there was no wrong way to do it? What might change in your life?

Share your art
@dreamupnowjournal
#dreamupnow.

I FEEL . . . ARGUMENTATIVE

intimidating others / feeling trapped / blaming /
starting fights / feeling misunderstood

Meet Ryan "Bodhi" Marcus

A shy and quiet teen, Bodhi struggled socially in high school. In the hallways, he often kept his head down and didn't say anything. "That's why I played sports, it was my outlet," he says. "I wasn't shy on the field with my peers." Bodhi began playing soccer at age six, in a suburb 30 minutes north of New York City. He is now a yogi and high school physical education teacher who created a class called PEACE (Physical Education and Cooperative Environment). Bodhi leads students in a warmup and cooldown involving yoga and meditation. During class, students decide individually what they want to do, by asking themselves: *What's a fun way for me to stay physically active?* They can work out alone or invite others to join them for volleyball, running, or whatever they prefer. "I want my students to do something for their fitness and health, not because their grade depends on it," he explains.

Bodhi has been a physical education teacher for 13 years and a boys' varsity soccer coach for 13 years; he also coached soccer to three- to five-year-olds for 8 years. He recently accepted a new position as an athletic coordinator and is responsible for all athletic teams at the high school level. Over his career, Bodhi has helped a high percentage of his soccer players get into college, with several earning scholarships. Many of Bodhi's past students return to speak with his current students. Bodhi is also a yogi and children's book author. He earned his bachelor of science degree in physical education at SUNY Cortland and received his master's in special education from Long Island University. Learn more about Bodhi on Instagram at @bodhimarcus.

Bodhi Shares

Most of my high school soccer players are first- or second-generation young men from Haiti, Guatemala, Honduras, El Salvador, Mexico, and several other countries. Very few come from a household with two parents. Most live here in the United States with mom, while dad is still working in their former country. I find that many of my players have a lot of responsibilities. They are concerned about being taken advantage of and will often argue. Some believe, "If I don't care, I won't hurt." Or they might think that if they don't really try, then no one will come down on them or make them feel unworthy. This was a new thing for me when I started teaching 12 years ago. I didn't know what students were going through, their problems and everyday life issues. As a teen, I had parental involvement and support, and my school was in the same country where I grew up. I've had to learn and grow in order to support my students.

There was once an athlete on my team who began to show more angry and combative emotions toward me and his teammates. One day after school he asked to talk privately with me before practice started. He opened up and told me about some problems he was having at home. He was worried his father and stepmother did not love him as much as his other siblings. He was feeling lost, unloved, and like his voice wasn't being heard. Listening to him opened my eyes. I didn't want to be just another adult who wasn't hearing his voice, who wasn't showing him love or giving him the guidance he desperately wanted. Talking to this young man, I remembered how it felt to be a teen who wasn't being heard and how I often felt like an outcast.

Together we came up with strategies for how to keep calm when the urge to argue or fight became overwhelming, like sitting quietly near the team to collect his thoughts. I'm also a big proponent of yoga and meditation. Sometimes teachers might assume students are being disrespectful because they have an "attitude problem" or because they are "just looking for trouble." If you're feeling misunderstood, I encourage you to find out what the root of the problem is and open an honest line of communication with an adult in your life who might be able to help. When my student trusted me, I learned a lesson that I carry with me in my classes and with my soccer team to this day: it's okay to show emotions, to let your guard down.

Don't give up, and try not to take things personally. Responding to anger with anger only makes more anger. Practice not attacking back. If you're in attack mode, go for a walk—just get away from the situation and think about the consequences your actions might have. If you punch someone or curse out a teacher, nothing positive will come from it. So find a quiet spot to cool down and ask yourself: *Why am I being so defensive? Why am I on guard? Why do I need to attack?* Think through the consequences aggression will bring. Then, think about another, more helpful behavior to get what you want.

If you need help managing your aggression, find an adult you can talk to or reach out to a hotline or app listed in the resource section at the end of this journal.

DREAM UP NOW

You're feeling argumentative. Why? I'm going to ask some questions on the following page, and I'd like you to take a moment to analyze each one and come up with some positive things you can do to feel better. As you consider different ways to handle a disagreement, instead of arguing or yelling (and getting yelled at or worse), I challenge you to try a positive behavior once and see what happens, just as an experiment. Maybe you won't like it, but maybe it will help. Take what works and make it better. Take what doesn't work and consider whether you were completely open, or if you are sure about what's really bugging you.

Advice I Wish I'd Had

"If you are true to yourself and have good intentions, it doesn't matter what others might think of you. Be authentic and real, hold your head up, and let other people's negativity roll off your shoulders."

—Bodhi Marcus

I Feel . . . Argumentative

Answer the following questions honestly. Refer to this page whenever you need to turn your focus away from aggressive or argumentative feelings. You can update your ideas, visualize your solutions, or simply breathe while choosing how and when to act differently.

Why am I feeling combative toward a specific person?

How can I handle this differently?

Is it really that person who is making me mad, or did something happen earlier?

How can I handle this differently?

Why does it bug me?

How can I handle this differently?

What's the root of the upset? TIP: It's often not how it looks on the surface.

How can I handle this differently?

What is it that's really upsetting me?

How can I handle this differently?

I FEEL . . . CHILL

slow to anger / being confident in yourself /
avoiding stress / acting as a peacemaker

Meet Ryan "Bodhi" Marcus

Most people know that yoga and meditation can help you feel positive and relaxed. If you are feeling chill, how do you hold onto it, with everything—good and bad—that is going on around you? The world is an unpredictable place, and every person is carrying around worries and concerns, including you. It's true that responding to anger with anger only makes more anger. But think about how much power you have to change your environment, and the people in it, if you're feeling relaxed and chill. Coach Bodhi shows you how to leverage your good feelings into making the world around you a better place. (For more about Bodhi, see page 160.)

Bodhi Shares

Congratulations! You're feeling relaxed and chill.

It's my goal as a teacher to help my students have more positive days. I might teach a great yoga session in P.E. class and leave my students feeling relaxed and good, but when they go back into the hallways at our high school, they immediately are bombarded with all the noise and the gossip and the crowds pushing in every direction. It's easy to feel calm one moment, and then suddenly someone shoves you, and you're ready to fight—all your relaxation gone.

Enjoy the relaxed feeling you have right now. When someone shoves you or does something upsetting, remain mindful, which means being deliberately aware of your body, mind, and feelings in the present moment. The person who shoved you might be having a crappy day. Notice the noise and pressure surrounding you, while focusing on being centered, relaxed, and compassionate with the many people around you who didn't have the opportunity you had to burn off some energy or challenging feelings. Your sense of being relaxed is something you own, and you don't want to give it away—or have it taken by someone who isn't as dialed in as you are.

If someone is ready to fight or argue with you, pause before you respond. If you call out an aggressive person in public, they will probably double down to show they won't be threatened. But if you remain centered and calm, you can just talk. You can de-escalate the situation by asking what's going on, quietly to one side. You might try asking something as simple as, "What would you like me to do?" When an overemotional person is amping up to fight, remaining calm and asking a simple question or two can help them switch gears and start using more evolved thinking skills.

Don't embarrass anyone by doing it publicly. Just show you care. Being positive and chill is contagious, just as being aggressive is. If you can help someone calm down, you can help them get to where they want to be emotionally. And, as you have more and more positive days, you'll attract more and more calm and chill people. You'll invite positive behaviors to you, just as the hotheaded fighter attracts violent outbursts. You are powerful in your calmness.

DREAM UP NOW

Make the most of feeling calm, chill, and positive by free-drawing. Free-drawing works in two ways. First, if you are already chill, drawing is an act of mindfulness, which means being fully aware of the present moment. You can draw simple shapes, characters, or whatever feels relaxing to you. Holding onto your positive vibe attracts others with a positive vibe to you. Second, if you are upset or riled up, free-drawing is an easy, quick way to calm down. All you have to do is breathe and draw. If you can harness your inner peace even when you're being provoked, you will make the world around you a better place.

Advice I Wish I'd Had
"Practice doesn't make perfect: it makes permanent."
—Bodhi Marcus

I Feel . . . Chill

Begin by drawing something easy and comfortable, then expand on it. There's no right or wrong. Personally, I have zero background with art. I was always a sports guy and never felt comfortable making art. No one ever taught me. I just draw what feels good. Recently, I've been drawing a little meditating Buddha-type guy. Or I'll draw a big sun or trees and grass.

You might choose symbols and see where that takes you. You can color them in, repeat patterns, whatever.

Free-drawing without rules helps you be mindful, helps you get inside your own head in a positive way. If your picture doesn't come out the way you want at first, just keep going and add to it. Try not to get frustrated, and just keep drawing. There is no suppression. Let go of the outcome and enjoy the experience.

Share your art
@dreamupnowjournal
#dreamupnow.

PATTERNS AND REFLECTIONS

Hey, look how far you've come. Take a moment to flip back through the activities you've completed so far. Do you see any patterns? Reflecting on where you've been can help lead you to where you want to go. Use this space to note things that keep coming up. You might see what time of day you have certain feelings, places you like (or avoid), which issues need the most attention, and which people lift you up—or bring you down.

Events

People

Places

Feelings

Words

Share your art
@dreamupnowjournal
#dreamupnow.

Recommended Resources

Crisis Hotlines and Emergency Support

Teen Line—Teens Helping Teens (1-800-TLC-TEEN / 1-800-852-8336). Confidential telephone line for teen callers, staffed by trained teen volunteers. Available 6–10 p.m. PST. (Text "TEEN" to 839863.) Visit teenlineonline.org.

National Suicide Prevention Lifeline (1-800-273-8255). Information, referrals, and suicide prevention counseling 24-7. Visit suicidepreventionlifeline.org.

RAINN National Sexual Assault Hotline (1-800-656-HOPE / 1-800-656-4673). A safe, anonymous way to learn how to get help after a sexual assault, 24-7. Visit rainn.org.

Poison Help Hotline (1-800-222-1222). Free, confidential, expert medical advice from toxicology professionals 24-7. Visit poisonhelp.org.

Child and Family Services. Every state has a free 800 number for child abuse reporting. Search "Department of Child and Family Services (DCFS)" for your state's number.

Online

MY3 app (my3app.org) helps you to create a network you can reach out to when you are feeling suicidal. A crisis prevention specialist is available to help 24-7.

Teen Talk (teenlineonline.org/teentalkapp) is a free iPhone app where you can go for support from a trained teen advisor. Available from 6–10 p.m. PST.

How-To Videos and Tutorials. Find online tutorials for each set of complementary dark and light emotions in your *Dream Up Now* guided journal. These how-to videos introduce you to us, author Rayne Lacko and contributing author Lesley Holmes, and give you a visual demonstration of the activities. Visit DreamUpNow.com to download.

About the Authors

Rayne Lacko is a Young Adult author and an advocate for the arts as a form of social and emotional well-being. Through her work, she inspires young people and their families to use creativity to stimulate positive change in their lives and communities.

Rayne resides on Bainbridge Island, near Seattle, Washington, with her spouse and two boys (a pianist and a drummer), a noisy cat, and her canine best friend. Learn more at RayneLacko.com.

Lesley Holmes contributes her expertise to several educational and arts nonprofits, helping children, teens, and older adults learn and heal through alternative therapies, music education, literacy, and food. She is a Los Angeles native who enjoys early morning hikes in the Hollywood Hills where she lives with her two teenage daughters.

Other Great Books from Free Spirit!

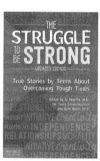

The Struggle to Be Strong
True Stories by Teens About
Overcoming Tough Times
(Updated Edition)
edited by Al Desetta, M.A.,
and Sybil Wolin, Ph.D.
For ages 13 & up.
184 pp.; PB; 6" x 9".

Fighting Invisible Tigers
Stress Management
for Teens
(Revised & Updated
4th Edition)
by Earl Hipp
For ages 11 & up.
144 pp.; PB; 2-color; illust.;
6" x 9".

Interested in purchasing multiple quantities and receiving volume discounts?
Contact edsales@freespirit.com or call 1.800.735.7323 and ask for Education Sales.

Many Free Spirit authors are available for speaking engagements, workshops, and keynotes. Contact speakers@freespirit.com or call 1.800.735.7323.

For pricing information, to place an order, or to request a free catalog, contact:

Free Spirit Publishing Inc. • 6325 Sandburg Road • Suite 100 • Minneapolis, MN 55427-3674
toll-free 800.735.7323 • local 612.338.2068 • fax 612.337.5050
help4kids@freespirit.com • freespirit.com